Liberalism

Liberalism

✦

Time-Tested Principles for the Twenty-First Century

E Pluribus Unum

Earl A. Reitan

iUniverse, Inc.

New York Lincoln Shanghai

Liberalism
Time-Tested Principles for the Twenty-First Century

iUniverse, Inc.

For information address:
iUniverse, Inc.
2021 Pine Lake Road, Suite 100
Lincoln, NE 68512
www.iuniverse.com

ISBN: 0-595-30369-2 (pbk)
ISBN: 0-595-76746-X (cloth)

Printed in the United States of America

To ordinary Americans, who make the United States a great country, and to Liberals, who strive to make it a good country for everyone.

Contents

Preface

My book is a work of passion, and I hope it arouses a similar passion in others, because without passion there will be no action.

The election of George W. Bush as president of the United States in the year 2000, marked the culmination of a forty-year assault on the liberal ideals that have shaped modern America. Bush and his advisers made no secret of their determination to dismantle the liberal policies that made America great.

During those two decades, Liberals became demoralized and tongue-tied. They were distracted by the Vietnam War and by new social issues. They lost sight of the time-tested principles of Liberalism. Now they leave the defense of their cause to professional politicians who are ready to sacrifice principles to careerism, or to strident advocates of minority and special interest complaints that do not resonate with ordinary Americans. They shun the word "Liberal" and adopt as an alternative the meaningless word "Progressive."

The United States led and still leads the world in the development of a capitalist democracy in an advanced society. Throughout the twentieth century, Liberals looked to the federal government to coordinate the various elements of our country into a functioning whole. Liberal presidents took the lead in implementing the ideals of Liberalism in peace and war. Under liberal leadership, the United States became the most successful country in the history of the world.

It is incredible that anyone would want to turn back the enormous achievements of American Liberalism. But that is what the people who call themselves "Conservatives" intend to do.

This book deals with Liberals and Conservatives, but references to the Democratic and Republican parties are inescapable. These organized political parties have been and remain the formal means by which Liberals and

Conservatives define their policies, mobilize voters, contest elections, and seek to achieve their goals.

Most Liberals were and still are Democrats. The Democratic Party became the majority party by leading the United States through the Great Depression of the 1930s and World War II. After the war, the Democrats took the lead in the Cold War, and came forward with new federal programs to meet important national needs. One reason for writing this book is to remind Democrats of the principles that made their party the dominant party in American politics for much of the twentieth century.

In the meantime, the Republican Party was changing. Although the Republican Party in the twentieth century has been primarily conservative, in the early part of the century it included an important contingent of liberal Republicans, of whom Theodore Roosevelt was the most notable. In the years after World War II, the party contained a strong liberal element, primarily from the East Coast.

The national Republican Party has now been taken over by extremists from the South, Southwest, the Mountain States, and California. Under Pres. George W. Bush they have taken this country on a reckless course of war and fiscal irresponsibility that will eventually destroy the liberal policies and programs that helped make America great. A second reason for writing this book is to urge sensible, moderate Republicans to reconsider their loyalty to a party that, on the national level, does not represent their views.

This book contains many references to "ordinary Americans," the bulk of the population and the bedrock of our country. These are Americans who are gainfully employed (or are retired), support their families, obey the laws, accept civic responsibilities, associate amicably with their colleagues, friends, neighbors, and relatives, and enjoy the common diversions and recreations of our time.

Ordinary Americans are extraordinary people: creative, energetic, and remarkably varied in their ethnic and social backgrounds. They look to government at all levels to provide leadership and essential services. In that sense, they are basically liberal. They keep an eye on their elected officials through the press and television, but they do not identify strongly with political philosophies or specific agendas. They leave big issues, such as foreign policy, public finance, and defense to their elected leaders. These extraordinary "ordinary Americans" are the people who make this country work.

The main reason for writing this book is to clarify for ordinary Americans the liberal ideas that were America's road map to greatness. Ordinary Americans are open to arguments that make sense. A tough-minded, realistic Liberalism that knows what it stands for will probably be successful politically, but providing a platform for electoral success is not the purpose of this book. If committed Liberals keep the time-tested principles of Liberalism in the public view, the politicians will be able to make the modifications and compromises that are necessary to make progress in a representative democracy. Getting Liberals back on track—and America back on track—is the ultimate purpose of this book.

This book has an historical dimension, because Liberalism has developed over time and the fundamental principles have been adapted to new circumstances as times changed. Historical perspective is also needed to prevent false analogies. Liberalism is not applicable to all times and places. Although liberal principles have wide applicability, Liberals need to be aware of the historical contingency of specific liberal policies.

Every book has a personal dimension too. I grew up in Minnesota, the grandson of Norwegian immigrants. My family struggled through the Depression, but managed to send me to Concordia College, Moorhead MN for one year before I entered the U. S. Army. I served in Italy and France as a rifleman with the Third Infantry Division. In 1946 I was honorably discharged and returned to Concordia College, where the GI Bill enabled me to complete my undergraduate degree in 1948. I went on to graduate study in history at the University of Illinois in 1948, and received the Ph.D. degree in History in 1954. Since that time I have taught American, English, and European History, and American Government at Illinois State University, Normal. In short, I am a Midwesterner, with the practical, down-to-earth perspective of the breed, and an heir to the Liberalism of Hubert Humphrey and Adlai Stevenson.

This book is not a scholarly book, although, as a university professor, I have published my quota of that kind of material. No footnotes or bibliography here. My book is a plea from the Heartland for a return to the time-tested principles of American Liberalism before it was corrupted by global power, swaggering militarism, electoral corruption, and the trivialization of public life by television.

A distinguished gentleman in our town liked to ask people: "What is your passion?" A penetrating question. Most people have strong commitments to their jobs, families, recreations and hobbies, communities, and their country. These are the elements of life, not passions.

My book is a work of passion, and I hope it arouses similar passions in others, because without passion there will be no action.

I wish to express my appreciation to my wife, Carol, and many good friends, among them Amos Miller, H. Loring White, G. Alan Hickrod, Ralph Bellas, and Walter Arnstein for their encouragement and suggestions. Publication of a hardback version in April 2004 provided an opportunity to revise and update the book.

Earl A. Reitan
Normal IL

1

Liberalism: What is it?

The liberal philosophy has become a driving force throughout the world. It is important to understand and cherish the liberal heritage and make it workable for the twenty-first century. At present, that responsibility falls heavily upon the United States and the American people.

The Philosophic Principles

Liberalism is a philosophy of government and society that emphasizes "Liberty," a word of great power down the ages. The word originally was applied to the special privileges of certain groups, as in the "liberties" of the nobles, or of provinces, or of the towns. In the sixteenth century, when the Dutch fought against Spanish rule, they said they were fighting for their "liberties"; the eventual outcome was independence. In this way Liberty came to be identified with freedom from rule by outsiders.

By the eighteenth century the word Liberty had taken on a second meaning: from independence or privileges for special groups to the rights of individuals. John Locke declared that the inherent rights of each individual were life, liberty, and property, which should be maintained by a government that received its power from the people. When Patrick Henry exclaimed "Give me Liberty or give me death," he used the word in both senses: he was claiming his personal freedom as an individual, but he was also asserting the freedom of the colony of Virginia from the alien and tyrannical (so he thought) rule of King George III.

The *Declaration of Independence* was based on both meanings of the word Liberty.

Liberal principles have a long pedigree going back to Greek democracy, Roman law, the Christian concern for the individual soul, Renaissance awareness of the worth of individual personality, and the Reformation emphasis on the relationship of the individual to God. In the seventeenth and eighteenth centuries these movements fused in the Enlightenment, which placed its confidence in reason and science as opposed to political, philosophical, or religious authorities.

Beginning in the seventeenth century, the main voices of Liberalism were English and American: Milton's defense of free expression in *Areopagitica*, *The Declaration of Rights*, Locke's advocacy of natural rights and the voice of the people, the *Declaration of Independence*, Adam Smith's *The Wealth of Nations*, and John Stuart Mill's *Principles of Political Economy, On Liberty, Considerations on Representative Government*, and *The Subjection of Women*.

French liberal thinkers of the eighteenth century, such as Voltaire and Montesquieu, were influenced by the example of Britain, although the classical heritage was important to them too. Their main concern was to limit the French monarchy by the rule of law. They did not have a strong parliamentary tradition to build on as a basis for representative government. French liberal thought culminated in the French Revolution and the *Declaration of the Rights of Man and the Citizen*.

The foundation of liberal thought is confidence in reason rather than reliance upon the authority of kings, priests, or dogmatic pronouncements of any kind. Liberalism welcomes a variety of views, but it is not agnostic. Essential to Liberalism is confidence that careful investigation and fair-minded assessment can achieve an approximation of truth adequate for ordinary purposes until new questions arise or new insights are gained. Liberals see reason as the only reliable guide to understanding ourselves and ordering our relationships with others.

Reason is an attribute of individuals, and consequently individualism has always been essential to Liberalism. Liberals wish to maximize the opportunities for individuals to make the most of their lives. They oppose all authoritarian or collectivist systems that subordinate the individual to some larger entity. Liberalism arose in opposition to divine-right monarchies, established churches, and tradition-bound societies, and Liberals continued their commitment to the freedom of individuals when challenged by Fascism, Nazism, and Communism.

Liberal individualism rests upon recognition of individual dignity. Liberals hold that individuals should be accepted as rational and responsible and worthy of respectful treatment unless they forfeit their claim through socially unacceptable behavior. Without denying differences of race, nationality, gender, or social class, Liberalism rests upon the foundation that each person should be regarded as worthy in his own right

Liberal individualism attaches to each person rights and responsibilities. Rights are those aspects of humanity that cannot be infringed by the larger society without some form of consent, usually expressed through a representative body. Responsibilities are those aspects of humanity that each individual can be expected to perform. Liberal thinkers reject special privileges and exemptions, except as established by law.

Given the liberal emphasis on individual dignity, it is not surprising that a major virtue in Liberalism is tolerance, since individuals vary greatly. Initially, the principle of tolerance was directed against the imposition of religious orthodoxies, but in a country as diverse as the United States tolerance became essential in other respects as well. By exercising tolerance, Liberal Democracy became workable in a country with great differences in geography, the ethnic and racial origins of its people, and wide disparities in wealth and education.

Modern Liberalism assumes a strong government that is actively involved in the national life. Liberals are not libertarians. Within that context, Liberals are committed to political equality, economic opportunity, and social justice. Liberals believe that every individual deserves a voice in the choice of political leaders and the shaping of public policy. Liberals expect government to provide a framework for economic growth, prepare individuals for employment, act positively to prevent blighted lives, and provide public amenities. Given the productivity of modern advanced economies, that is hardly an unreasonable goal.

Some critics charge that Liberalism offers no high and noble ideals—that modern Liberalism is nothing more than a desire for a comfortable existence in a consumer-oriented society. Undoubtedly there is a tendency in this age of consumerism to put too much emphasis on a fine house and car, the latest technological gadgets, and piling up money. And the rootless individual drifting through life is certainly a part of all advanced societies.

While adequate provision for the material needs of life is a goal of all liberal countries, there is much more to Liberalism than that. Liberalism has always had as its purpose a higher form of personal fulfillment, including meaningful relationships with other individuals and significant involvement in the larger community. Liberal societies have produced a remarkable flowering of scholarship, science, and the arts, and a popular culture of great power and creativity. At the root of these achievements lies liberty.

Liberalism has always had to maintain a balance between Liberal Idealism and the realities of the world as it is. While Liberals have always held high expectations for government, society, and individuals, the wisest Liberals have been Liberal Realists, who recognize the human, institutional, and cultural limitations within which Liberals must live and work.

The liberal philosophy has become a driving force throughout the world. It is important to understand and cherish the liberal heritage and make it workable for the twenty-first century. At present, that responsibility falls heavily upon the United States and the American people.

2

Political Liberalism

The principal concern of Liberalism has always been good government, which Liberals regard as an essential element of a good society.

Liberalism and the State

The term "the state" refers to the structure of authority that exercises sovereign power over the people within its territory. [Due to its federal structure, the word "state" has a somewhat different meaning in the United States.] Liberalism grew out of resistance to states that were autocratic and arbitrary. Although the state originated under the rule of kings or small privileged groups, Liberals insisted that the state derived its powers from the people and should exercise those powers for the benefit of the people.

For that reason, an important part of Liberalism is responsible citizenship. The liberal concept of political freedom and rights always posited citizens who were worthy of them. For states whose citizens lacked personal and public virtue, conflict leading eventually to anarchy or despotism was seen as the likely outcome.

The principal concern of Liberalism has always been good government, which Liberals regard as an essential element of a good society. Liberals were advocates of a government of restricted powers, for they saw government as a potential threat to Liberty, likely to become involved in wars, a place of privilege for politicians and their friends, and an expensive institution to maintain. At the same time, they recognized the importance of a strong government to defend the country against outside invasion or internal disorder. John Stuart Mill argued that a strong state was essential to freedom, for only strong government could protect individuals against intimidation or exploitation by the rich and powerful. Liberalism should not be confused with Libertarianism. Limited government, not weak government, is an essential principle of Liberalism.

The Development of Liberal Government

Liberalism developed in Britain as the means to maintain a strong and active government that could defend the nation, foster trade, and protect property without threatening Liberty. The means chosen was to limit government by law and representative institutions (i.e., Parliament). Democracy came gradually, as the King, Lords and Commons gave way to popular pressures. The franchise was extended to most of the middle class in the Reform Bill of 1832, and the Reform Bills of 1867 and 1884 established virtual manhood suffrage. (Women received the right to vote in 1918.) Led by William E. Gladstone, the Liberal Party grew out of this age of reform as the party of democracy, efficiency and economy in government, low taxes, free trade, a strong currency, and restraint in foreign and imperial policy. Despite Gladstone's efforts, the Liberal Party foundered on the intractable problems of Ireland, but took on new vitality at the turn of the century.

American Liberalism is rooted in the British liberal heritage. Our founding fathers took what they knew—British government—and modified it to serve their own purposes. They replaced the King with the President, the House of Lords with the Senate, and the House of Commons with the House of Representatives. Election (direct or indirect) replaced hereditary power. They rejected the British principle that officers of the executive branch (like the British Prime Minster and Cabinet) could also be members of the legislative branch. They explicitly prohibited two characteristics of British government: an hereditary nobility and an established church. Like the British, the Americans were devoted to the rule of law, and they established an independent federal judiciary to enforce federal laws and decide constitutional conflicts.

Shortly after ratification, the *Bill of Rights* was added to the Constitution in the form of ten amendments that protected individuals against abuse of power by the new government. Although many democracies exist in the world, no other country has a document equal to our *Bill of Rights,* or a court system and people as committed to civil rights as ours. Liberalism means civil liberties guaranteed by the rule of law.

American Liberalism was democratic almost from the beginning. In colonial times the right to vote was based on the possession of property, and in the American colonies property ownership was widespread. In the new American republic, citizenship was the privilege of responsible, property-owning, tax-paying individuals, and such persons were (and still are) the bedrock of American society. By the Age of Jackson the advance of democracy had extended the right to vote to virtual manhood suffrage, although women and slaves were still excluded.

The great anomaly in American government ended with the Civil War and the abolition of slavery. While the states of the Confederacy were out of the union, the liberal thrust of American politics was greatly advanced by ratification of the Thirteenth, Fourteenth, and Fifteenth amendments. These amendments guaranteed the former slaves full political and civil rights, including the right to vote. The Fourteenth Amendment strengthened civil liberties by applying the principles of the *Bill of Rights* to the states, and making enforcement a role of the federal courts. Adherence to these amendments was shamefully evaded for a century, and the civil rights movement of the 1960s was needed to make the force of law effective in all parts of the country.

Not until after World War I did women receive the right to vote. The Fourteenth Amendment stated that no state could deprive "any person" of the "equal protection of the laws." In its wisdom, the U. S. Supreme Court decided that the word "person" applied to corporations but not to women, a violation of common sense that eventually led to the unsuccessful Equal Rights Amendment. In actuality, the course of events in recent years has given women pretty much what they had a right to expect under the "equal protection" clause or what they might have obtained from the Equal Rights Amendment.

The American Presidency

The key to modern American Liberalism has been its reliance upon a strong presidency to achieve liberal goals. The executive is the mainspring of all modern governments. Modern Liberals have been advocates of presidential leadership, because Liberals are people of action, and the Presidency embodies the power to act. The President brings to his office the authority of popular election. He is the leader of our country in its foreign relations, Commander-in-Chief of the world's most powerful military forces, chief executive of a large administrative structure, and responsible for the expenditure of a huge budget. The President is (or should be) the tribune of the people, with his base in his role as spokesman for the nation and his access to the "bully pulpit" of the media.

In many respects, our Presidents have failed us badly in the past four decades. "Power tends to corrupt," Lord Acton sagely observed, a principle well-understood by our Founding Fathers, who attempted to guard against it through a system of checks and balances. Presidential theatre, television politics, and a vast executive patronage have weakened the role of Congress as a check and balance on presidential power in the intoxicating realms of foreign policy, defense, and war. Congress and the President collaborate in budgetary matters to provide benefits to their constituents and contributors at the expense of the American people.

Democracy in the United States has been profoundly changed by radio and television, which dominate political campaigns and elections. The enormous cost of advertising in the broadcast media has made politicians dependent upon large contributors and has corrupted the functioning of representative government. Electoral reform at all levels must be a major concern of Liberals, whether they benefit politically or not. At the moment, campaign money dominates presidential and Congressional elections. That must be changed. Only Liberals are likely to advocate campaign reform that will remove politics from the media hucksters and still give candidates and advocacy groups opportunities to bring their ideas before the public.

The Federal-State Partnership

A distinctive feature of American government is our federal system, a necessary arrangement when the constitution was adopted, and still a valuable part of our national structure. Federal powers are specified in the constitution and all other powers remain with the states, a principle re-enforced by the mysterious Tenth Amendment. Federal powers, however, have been vastly expanded under the commerce clause and later amendments. State and local governments have also expanded their responsibilities to meet the needs of an advanced society.

Liberals have done some of their most effective work at the state and local levels, which was the distinctive contribution of the Progressive Movement of the early twentieth-century. In addition to reform of state and local governments to make them honest and efficient, the Progressives realized that state and local governments had to act positively to improve education and cope with social disarray. This principle has become an important element in American Liberalism.

While working with state and local governments, a consistent feature of American Liberalism has been readiness to seek national solutions to national problems. The great problems of our country are national in scope and require national (sometimes international) solutions. These problems will not go away by delegating them to the states, and fifty different ways of dealing with these problems can only create chaos.

Education is a state and local responsibility, but federal financial support is essential to promote excellence and maintain minimum standards nationwide. It has become clear that the problems of health care must be resolved on a national basis. Much of the effort to protect the environment requires federal action, although there is certainly considerable room for state and local initiatives to deal with their special problems. Most crime is a matter for states and localities, but strong federal support certainly is helpful, especially in dealing with organized crime, which does not respect state lines. Immigration and race relations call for federal action, as does the problem of chronic, long-term poverty. Protection of people and property against terrorism requires federal coordination with state and local authorities.

Strong and active state and local governments are an essential element in Liberalism. Too often, Liberals have advocated large federal programs administered by a federal bureaucracy. Bill Clinton rejected this approach when he said "the age of big government is over." Perhaps Alice Rivlin, Director of the Congressional Budget Office, said it best when she commented: "The federal government should write the big checks and let the state and local governments write the little checks."

The Citizen in the Information Age

It is a truism that cannot be stated too often that Liberal Democracy depends on an informed citizenry. In recent years, the Internet has created a powerful new medium of communication that is having a profound effect on government and politics. A wide variety of newspapers, periodicals, and personal websites are available to people who are willing and able to use them. Political candidates, pressure groups, and affinity groups (businessmen, farmers, academics, veterans, evangelical Christians) use the Internet to communicate with targeted audiences. This method of communication becomes personalized as individuals use E-Mails to transmit articles, jokes, and personal comments to their friends. The Internet has become an important alternative to the commercialized mass media, and it is likely that this trend will continue.

Internet communications have already created a new political class—the cyberspace literates. They are exposed to a level of information and argumentation that differs from the mass media. Will the cyberspace literates hold the balance of power between the major political parties? Will they bring a level of knowledge and opinion into our political process, which has been so degraded by network and cable television and talk radio? Or will the Internet intensify partisanship? Liberals must use this powerful new tool to advance their principles and support candidates who can be expected to convert their principles into action.

3

Liberal Nationalism

Liberals have a tradition of Nationalism. If they wish to flourish again, Liberals must find leaders and spokesmen who can win the confidence of those ordinary Americans who consider the well being of America as their primary concern.

The Origins of Nationalism

Liberalism in the United States and elsewhere cannot be understood without attention to its close relative, Nationalism. Nationalism has been and still is a powerful force in the world. Sometimes Nationalism can be a force for evil, with Adolph Hitler as the most spectacular example. Sometimes Nationalism can be an ennobling force, as seen in the leadership of Winston Churchill and the sturdy determination of the British people during World War II.

The root of Nationalism is primitive tribalism, a visceral sense of the solidarity of a group of people against other peoples. In the Darwinian struggle of pre-historic times, tribalism was essential to survival. Outsiders were seen as threatening, and those dissidents who did not fit into the tribe were driven out.

With the growth of cities, the tribe metamorphosed into the community, variously defined. The Greeks gave primary loyalty to the city-state (the *polis*), but they also identified Hellas, the community of Greeks wherever they might live. They distinguished carefully between Hellenes and barbarians, even though the barbarian might be a cultivated Persian and the Hellene might be an ignorant Greek sailor. They recognized the importance of language and culture in shaping a community.

On the other hand, the Roman Empire saw itself as universal, as did the Christian Church. St. Paul wrote of a Christian community in which there was "neither Jew nor Greek, Goth nor Scythian, but all are in Christ."

Nationalism as it developed in Europe was exclusive. Nationalists cherished language and culture as badges of distinctiveness that separated them from other nations, which were often viewed as enemies. In England, France, and Spain, a strong state developed first, and Nationalism grew up (or was imposed) within the pre-existing political structure. Germany and Italy were politically fragmented, and the peoples of Eastern Europe were under the Prussian, Austrian, Russian, and Turkish empires. In those areas Nationalism began as a cultural identification and then became political. Nationalists claimed that people who felt themselves to be a nation (the new tribe) should be organized as a sovereign state. Eventually national goals were achieved, either by a process of unification that brought together separate states, as in Germany and Italy, or by throwing off imperial rule, as Nationalism grew among the peoples of the Austrian Empire and the Empire of the Turks.

At first, Nationalism also had strong liberal leanings. Liberal Nationalists insisted that the national state should be liberal in its principles and structure. In the first half of the nineteenth century, Liberal Nationalism became a powerful force on the European continent, as Liberals attempted to achieve constitutional government and national unity. The failure of the Liberal Nationalists in the Revolutions of 1848–49 marked a turning point in Central and Eastern Europe.

Liberal Nationalism was replaced by an authoritarian, militaristic form of Nationalism that sought to achieve national goals by illiberal means. Otto von Bismarck, the "Iron Chancellor" of Prussia proclaimed: "Not by speeches and majority resolutions are the great questions of the time decided—that was the mistake of 1848 and 1849—but by blood and iron." Bismarck used war to unify Germany. He established in the heart of Europe a powerful nation-state based on authoritarianism and militarism. Italy tagged along in a similar manner. In 1867 the Austrian Empire gave a high degree of independence to the Hungarians, thus gaining their support in holding the empire together against other subordinate nationalisms. The czars of Russia used Nationalism, Orthodox Christianity, and repression to keep Liberalism at bay, but Nicholas II had to yield to liberal forces in the October Constitution of 1905. One by one, Greece, Rumania, Bulgaria, and Serbia threw off the Turkish yoke.

Before World War I, Liberalism was gaining ground in Germany, Italy, and Russia. After the war, liberal governments were short-lived. As the war was ending the Russian Empire collapsed, and the Communists, led by Lenin, seized power and established a party dictatorship. In 1923 Benito Mussolini, a Fascist, took power in Italy. Between 1929 and 1933 the Weimar Republic of Germany broke down, opening the door to Hitler and Nazism. Throughout Central and Eastern Europe, Liberalism was swept aside by Fascism, Communism, and other ideologies that denied the liberal concept of the importance of the individual and emphasized the authority of the state.

In Central Europe some strong advocates of liberal ideals of personal freedom remained until forced to flee. In 1941, Erich Fromm, a German psychoanalyst, published a book entitled *Escape from Freedom,* in which he explained the pathology of totalitarianism. Friedrich von Hayek, an Austrian political economist who had fled to London, wrote *The Road to Serfdom* (1944) to advocate personal freedom and free-market principles.

Liberalism and Nationalism in the United States

In the United States, Liberalism and Nationalism have always gone hand in hand, but sometimes the relationship has been an uneasy one. While Liberalism emphasizes freedom, Nationalism emphasizes unity and order. The Revolutionary War stimulated both liberal and national impulses, and led to a constitution that was both liberal and national. Emerson and Whitman proclaimed that an American national culture was emerging, based on the European inheritance but fresh and distinctive, displaying the vitality of a new nation.

The Lincoln administration fought a terrible civil war to establish the principle that the United States was one nation, whether the states of the Confederacy liked it or not. The Thirteenth, Fourteenth, and Fifteenth amendments advanced American Liberal Nationalism by extending federal jurisdiction over the states to guarantee civil rights. After the Civil War, American national unity was advanced by the growth of industry and the building of railroads. The telegraph and telephone created a national communications network. The public schools undertook the task of Americanizing the flood of immigrants. Steam-powered presses made newspapers and books affordable, and the Post Office and rural free delivery made them available to all.

In the twentieth century, liberal programs were justified, to some extent, by the need to preserve the unity of our country. Franklin D. Roosevelt's New Deal was national in that it was offered as an antidote to social conflict of the kind that was breaking out elsewhere. World War II was a great national effort dedicated to liberal goals. After World War II, Presidents Harry Truman, John F. Kennedy, and Lyndon Johnson strengthened national unity with programs that increased opportunities and reduced economic deprivation and social injustices. The Interstate Highway System, begun under Pres. Dwight D. Eisenhower, was advocated as important to national defense, but its role in binding our country together economically and through travel is obvious. The Civil Rights Movement was national, in that its purpose was to strengthen the unity of our country by bringing African-Americans into the mainstream of American life. Martin Luther King was not only a great American Liberal. He was an American Nationalist as well.

Liberal Nationalism and the Vietnam War

The Vietnam War was the great crisis of American Liberal Nationalism. The war was initiated and escalated by liberal presidents. John F. Kennedy committed our national honor and Lyndon Johnson committed our national power. Eloquent liberal spokesmen, among them Vice-President Hubert Humphrey, Secretary of State Dean Rusk, and Secretary of Defense Robert McNamara portrayed the war as a crusade to advance liberal democracy and national independence in Southeast Asia. American Conservatives, powerfully influenced by militarism, joined in support and eventually became the strongest advocates of that terrible self-inflicted wound. At the beginning few doubted that the United States had the military power to accomplish its mission.

Although liberal presidents had led the nation into the Vietnam War, it was also the Liberals who challenged it and provided the major opposition. Liberals on the Senate Foreign Relations Committee, led by U. S. Senator J. William Fulbright, incurred the wrath and vengeance of Pres. Johnson by arguing that the war did not benefit the United States, did not advance freedom and democracy in Vietnam, and did not contribute to stabilizing the emerging world community. It was the Liberals who denounced sending American troops into a war that served no national purpose. Theirs was the truly patriotic position. They claimed the right of citizens in a democracy to criticize the policies of the government, especially when the policies were so evidently damaging to the country.

The anti-war Liberals faced a hard choice: support their government (including its military forces) in its slide into disaster, or stand up against the government for the wellbeing of the nation. For most people the government and the nation were one and the same, and opposition to a war, once the commitment was made, was seen as a betrayal of our military forces. That is why the anti-war Liberals could never make their case with the public.

The Liberals who opposed the war were charged with being unpatriotic, a charge used by Presidents Johnson and Nixon to maintain public support for a war that they knew they could not win. The Conservatives claimed to be the patriots, waved American flags, and stigmatized the Liberals as "pointy-headed, effete intellectual snobs" or raffish potheads. The American tribal instinct had been aroused, and rationality was cast to the winds. Those whose willfulness and ignorance had led the nation into the war, or who prolonged it, as Nixon did, beat the tom-toms of Nationalism. The great majority of Americans, bewildered by the argument, wrapped themselves in the American flag and hoped for the best.

The abuse of Nationalism to support a bad cause led to a reaction against Nationalism among some Liberals—a distortion of Liberalism with damaging effects. Liberals were justified in criticizing the wisdom and conduct of the war, but a strident "New Left" appeared that impugned the very principles, character, and culture of the nation. In so doing, they discredited mainstream Liberalism and left a bitter aftertaste that still remains. Ever since the Vietnam War, patriotism has been claimed as the special preserve of Conservatives and confused in the public mind with militarism and war.

Liberals have failed in that they have not presented a nationalist message that gives the highest priority to maintaining the strength and vitality of the United States and the wellbeing of the American people. Liberal Nationalists know that a democracy that exercises world leadership must be strong at home. Ignorance, poverty, crime and racism in the United States damage our country and weaken the democratic message that America offers to the rest of the world. When the Puritans settled in New England their goal was to be a beacon—"a city set on a hill." Liberal adherence to this noble goal is the highest form of patriotism.

Liberal Internationalism

In our own time the growing interdependence of the peoples of the world has led to another aspect of Liberalism: Liberal Internationalism. While accepting the importance and value of the national state, American Liberals have always maintained a sense of peoples and nations as part of a larger human community. Liberal presidents, Woodrow Wilson and Franklin D. Roosevelt, led America in two world wars dedicated to the advancement of democracy. Wilson led in the establishment of the League of Nations, and Roosevelt the United Nations Organization. Pres. Harry Truman demonstrated the liberal faith in democracy by committing America to the Cold War.

It is time to expose the internationalist mission to a strong dose of Liberal Realism. John F. Kennedy proclaimed: "we shall pay any price, bear any burden, meet any hardship, support any friend, oppose any foe, to assure the survival and success of liberty." Although that message may have had some relevance in the days of the Cold War, since that time presidential egos, electoral politics, unrealistic hopes, and exaggerated fears have led to excesses that endanger the long-term strength of the great liberal undertaking that is the United States of America. Television, which requires conflict and human interest (preferably in exotic locales) to sell fast food and over-the-counter medicines, contributes to this misdirection of national resources.

When Liberals adopt a Messianic concept of America's destiny to spread freedom and democracy throughout the world, they overlook the wide differences between nations and cultures and the intractability of most of the world's problems. Many local and regional crises are not resolvable by American intervention, no matter how well intended. Liberal Realism calls for great discrimination in undertaking such involvements. Liberals should remember the old adage: "The road to Hell is paved with good intentions."

Liberals must maintain the American commitment to international cooperation in the resolution of disputes between nations and blocs of nations, but with a realistic assessment of what can be accomplished and the cost. The United Nations has great prestige throughout the world as an arbiter of international conflicts and as a sponsor of interventions in disturbed areas. That is an important role and should be respected. The shortcomings of the United Nations are all too apparent. The organization is not united, and some of its members are travesties of nations. Some powerful countries, like Germany and Japan, are not members of the Security Council but should be. Nevertheless, it is especially important that the world organization be brought into any decision to wage war or become involved in civil strife. and the views expressed there should be seriously considered, although not regarded as determinative.

Given the flaws of the United Nations, Americans may as well accept the reality that a stable world order depends on them and their allies among the advanced countries. America and its allies should expect, from time to time, to use military force judiciously to maintain peace and stability. Pres. George H. Bush obtained United Nations approval and the support of allies to repulse Saddam Hussein's invasion of Kuwait. Pres. Bill Clinton obtained the approval of the United Nations and worked with allies to stop "ethnic cleansing" in Bosnia and Kosovo

George W. Bush plunged into war in Iraq unilaterally, despite widespread disapproval by our allies and within the United Nations. The contemptuous attitude of the Bush administration toward world opinion now comes back to haunt them as they plead for help in Iraq. Most of the nations of the world will work with the United States to maintain a peaceful and stable world order. But we must be ready to work with them and concede that their judgments should play a part in any decision to use military force. We must work with international institutions, our allies, and other countries to make a better and safer world community, but we must not mortgage America's future while doing it.

E Pluribus Unum and Civic Nationalism

Liberals are instinctively tolerant of differences and sympathetic to a wide range of cultures. Nevertheless, the time has come for Liberals to concern themselves with national unity. Our national motto is *e pluribus unum*: out of many, one. This motto originally referred to our federal union and the relationship between the federal government and the states. As regional, ethnic, and cultural differences mount, it becomes increasingly important to preserve the *unum* in our motto.

American Nationalism was never like the "blood and soil" Nationalisms of Europe, which claimed ethnic unity and deeply rooted ties to the land. American Nationalism can best be termed Civic Nationalism, for it is based on commitment to our constitution and laws and loyalty to the United States above all other countries. Civic Nationalism recognizes that the rights and processes of a free country can be exercised only within the boundaries of a sovereign national state. American Civic Nationalism leaves ample room for a wide variety of organizations and cultural and religious interests. Competence in the use of the English language is not essential, but it is difficult to be a good citizen without it.

Perhaps the most important venues for strengthening American Civic Nationalism are the schools and universities. It is important to maintain America as a civilization with a set of ideals and institutions that bind Americans together despite their differences. There is a trend in American higher education to emphasize the history and continuing problems of privilege, political corruption, corporate greed, poverty, race, ethnicity, gender, and social class. Although these problems certainly were and are real and should be ventilated, the traditional American story told how these problems were dealt with and surmounted in the interest of the greater good.

Liberals have a tradition of Nationalism. If they wish to flourish again, Liberals must find leaders and spokesmen who can win the confidence of those ordinary Americans who consider the well being of America as their primary concern.

4

Conservatism

The challenge to Liberals is to demonstrate to ordinary Americans that a realistic but forward-looking Liberalism will best conserve the gains of the past and meet the needs of the future.

Conservatism: The European Model

The United States is and always has been a highly dynamic country. With a great continent to settle and develop, and a creative and energetic people, change has been the essence of American life. Liberals are willing to lead and manage change, and for that reason the liberal tradition is at the heart of American history. In the United States, Conservatives inevitably found themselves sitting on the sideline, viewing with alarm, as America grew into a great nation.

Europe, with a much longer history, developed strong conservative philosophies that have had little influence in the United States. What is called "Conservatism" in this country is, by European standards, not conservative at all.

The process by which Liberalism became dominant in the advanced countries of Europe, was, of course, resisted by people of different outlook and temperament. Liberalism was identified with the middle class, who saw their aspirations frustrated by the privileges of the upper ranks of society. These middle-class liberals believed that they deserved political and social recognition, since their talents and energy were the creative elements in society and the wave of the future.

Conservatives, by definition, were more interested in conserving what existed, especially if it was good for them, than in taking the risks of change. Conservatism was a viewpoint fostered by elites in government, the Church, and society, but conservative views also appealed to many ordinary people, who were respectful toward their betters and resistant to things new.

Historically, British and European Conservatives looked to strong governments as a necessary check upon the impulsiveness and irresponsibility of the people—"the many-headed monster in the public square." They advocated government by elites, who alone were considered capable of making wise decisions. British and continental Conservatives were determined to preserve an hierarchical society, with prestige and power moving from the top downward. They claimed that most people wanted the security of a well-ordered community more than individual freedom and political participation.

If one seeks the intellectual foundations of modern Conservatism, the place to begin is with Edmund Burke—Irish by birth, English by choice, a Whig in politics. Burke argued that timely and moderate reform was true Conservatism. In addition to political and financial reform, he advocated relaxing the laws that gave privileges to the Church of England and restricted religious freedom for Catholics and Protestant dissenters. He pointed out the importance of responding constructively to the complaints of the people before things got out of hand.

Burke opposed the efforts of George III and his ministers to suppress the American colonists by force. He regarded it as impracticable (which it proved to be), and he argued that the colonists were standing up for what they believed to be the rights of Englishmen. He attacked the abuse of British power in Ireland and India; he advocated responsible and humane government in dependent colonies; he criticized the slave trade and brutal criminal laws and prisons; he advocated many other forward-looking reforms that would justify the rule of the elite by improving English law and society.

When the French Revolution broke out in 1789, Burke supported the Crown, the Church, and the Tory Party (the Conservatives), because he saw in France the excesses of popular government without constitutional restraints. Even at this time his actions were liberal, for his purpose was to preserve constitutional government, parliamentary institutions, and freedom under law against democratic rabble-rousing and popular dictatorship.

Burke's Conservatism was cultural as well as political: he admired the cultural heritage of Europe and wished to support cultural and religious institutions that had been developed and refined over centuries. His conservative philosophy was the opposite of the views of those modern Americans who call themselves Conservatives. Burke wanted to preserve and improve existing institutions, not tear them down. He was well informed on economic matters, and he saw economic policy in terms of the welfare of the community, not an individual scramble for gain. He respected social classes as part of a natural order, although (as an Irishman and a commoner) he had known the indignities that social superiors can inflict on ambitious men of talent.

In the reign of Queen Victoria the British Conservative Party developed a tradition of "Tory Democracy," which meant that upper-class elites would justify their power and wealth by appealing to the urban working class. Benjamin Disraeli, Conservative Prime Minister, found that people could be excited by showy foreign policy involvements in Europe, and by colonial wars in far-off places like southern Africa and Afghanistan, that graveyard of invaders. He also advocated measures to improve public health and housing in Britain's teeming industrial cities. After World War II, when Winston Churchill was the leader of the Conservative Party, he supported the Labour Party's social programs. The Conservatives maintained a tradition of paternalism until Margaret Thatcher took the party in another direction.

There is a place in the American political spectrum for a social and cultural Conservatism on the British model. Responsible American Conservatives should develop their own "Tory Democracy" and insist that those who are well off assume greater responsibility for those who are not. Conservatives should work to see that American civilization and the institutions that sustain it are strengthened. This kind of Conservatism, however, found no place in the vulgar individualism and greed of *The Contract with America*.

Political Conservatism in America

What about Conservatism in America?

When our national government was established, the Federalists, to whom Americans owe their magnificent constitution, assumed the role of an elite. "The people who own the country should run it," declared John Jay, the first Chief Justice of the U. S. Supreme Court. The Federalists ran afoul of American's growing democracy and sectional tensions and disappeared from the scene, as stand-pat Conservatism usually does.

The Whigs tried to straddle the fence and reconcile the irreconcilable—the sectional differences between the North and the South that were rooted in slavery. They, too, disappeared, as Conservatives invariably do when they avoid dealing with fundamental problems. A former Whig, Abraham Lincoln, a man of courage and conviction, joined the new Republican Party and eventually excised the cancer that had divided America, albeit at enormous cost.

In the early decades of the twentieth century American Conservatism was the domain of the Republican Party, but the rise of the United States to a major power brought with it impulses toward change. Pres. Theodore Roosevelt and the Progressive Movement exercised a positive role within the Republican Party and the nation. Pres. Herbert Hoover, a man of greater enlightenment and humanity than most of his fellow Republicans, struggled unsuccessfully to apply Republican doctrines to an unprecedented calamity, the Great Depression.

With Pres. Franklin D. Roosevelt and the New Deal, the Democratic Party, led by Liberals, became dominant. The Republicans, fuming on the sidelines, complained about New Deal efforts to mitigate the effects of the Depression and were isolationist in regard to the aggressions of Hitler in Europe. After the war the Democrats, led by Pres. Harry Truman, extended the New Deal social welfare measures, and took bold steps to stop Soviet expansion and the spread of Communism in Western Europe. The Republicans complained that the federal government was too large and taxes were too high. They accused the Democrats of expanding the government to increase the patronage and perpetuate their grip on power.

In the election of 1952, the Republicans gained the White House by capitalizing on the popularity of Gen. Dwight D. Eisenhower, a moderate Conservative. The Eisenhower administration was conservative in that it preserved most of the changes of its liberal predecessors, but there was clearly a different tone and emphasis. Balancing the budget—a necessary corrective to the activism of the previous twenty years—took precedence over full employment or meeting social needs. Nevertheless, the size and activity of the federal government continued to increase. Valuable new federal projects, such as the Interstate Highway System and airport construction, were undertaken. Eisenhower warned, in vain, against the increasing cost of "the military-industrial complex."

After Eisenhower, Republicans continued to speak the rhetoric of smaller government and lower taxes, but they expanded the size and cost of the federal government anyway. The most important single factor in the growth of government under Pres. Richard Nixon was foreign policy and defense (primarily the Vietnam War), but for some unknown reason Republicans have never counted defense as part of the growth of government. The Nixon administration was also active in expanding federal social programs. In addition to Amtrak, the Nixon administration established the Environmental Protection Agency, the Occupational Safety and Health Administration (OSHA), and quotas for hiring minorities under federal contracts.

Presidents Gerald Ford, the Conservative, and Jimmy Carter, the Liberal, were probably the best presidents since Eisenhower in terms of personal character and devotion to good government. They were buffeted by so many economic problems that their political philosophies became irrelevant. They were scorned by a restless, TV-driven public that craved flair, charm, and excitement. After leaving office they worked together productively on a number of joint assignments, and Carter gained distinction as an elder statesman and global trouble-shooter.

During those years, some conservative intellectuals were developing radical alternatives to the moderation of Eisenhower and Ford. They argued that the Republicans would never win if they were seen as a "me too" version of the Democrats. The Conservatives established think tanks, like the Cato Institute and the Heritage Foundation, to generate new ideas and research topics of potential political interest.

Conservative intellectuals challenged conventional Liberalism on several fronts. One group espoused a communitarian view that was found predominantly among literary idealists and religious thinkers. They detested capitalism and the consumer economy and looked back with longing to the strong communities that they imagined had existed before the age of affluence and self-indulgence. Some of these social Conservatives, like Michael Novak, were advocates of the urban working class, whose ethnicity and traditional family values they thought—with some justification—had been unfairly disparaged by haughty Liberals. They were reinforced by a reaction against the social changes of the 1960s, and were active opponents of abortion, an issue that suddenly sprang to life in the 1970s.

Other conservative thinkers took a reverse view: they were libertarians who argued that government and other agencies of community were stifling American individualism and were a threat to personal freedom and economic growth. They objected to the readiness of Liberals to prescribe policies and programs to shape a society that met liberal standards of fairness. Their views were expressed in the novels of Ayn Rand and Barry Goldwater's *The Conscience of a Conservative* (1960).

The third form of Conservatism advocated a powerful federal government and military forces to conduct ideologically based anti-Communist crusades around the world. These Conservatives were especially distressed by liberal opposition to the Vietnam War, which they attributed to inherent sympathy with Communism, the prevailing consumerism and hedonism, and a lack of self-discipline in the younger generation growing out of the child-raising principles of Dr. Spock.

American Conservatism gained a lively spokesman in 1951 with the publication of William F. Buckley's *God and Man at Yale.* Buckley's Conservatism was mainly negative and consisted largely of bashing Liberals and the excesses of the counter-culture. He was witty and persistent, and his magazine, *The National Review* (1956), became a popular outlet for conservative views. In the 1960s Buckley found himself riding a tide; his television program, "Firing Line," and a syndicated column were widely disseminated.

Apart from attacking Liberalism, Buckley's main influence was to claim philosophical and religious roots for the new Conservatism. Buckley's philosophizing and personal charm impressed some of the graduates pouring out of America's universities and colleges, who, in the usual fashion of young people, wanted to be different from their liberally oriented parents. It must be said that the emphasis of *The National Review* on thoughtful reviews of serious books gave some validity to the intellectual claims of the new Conservatives.

In the 1970s, these various forms of Conservatism merged into Reaganism, a political movement that masked its contradictions with the personal charm and rhetorical skills of a movie star and the new political techniques of media politics. Ronald Reagan was a man of ability and charm, who grew up in a struggling family in small-town Illinois and went to Hollywood where he had a successful career in the movies. He was always interested in politics, and went on to become Governor of California for two terms. In 1980 Ronald Reagan proved to be the greatest political campaigner since Franklin D. Roosevelt; his personal charm and effective speechmaking won him widespread popularity and the presidency. His legions of admirers claimed that he had slain the dragon of Liberalism and had made Conservatism the dominant force in American politics.

Intellectually, Reaganism was a muddled blending of political expediency, Cold War rhetoric, media hype, and a stew of the various conservative viewpoints. Polls consistently showed that the majority of Americans disagreed with Reagan on the issues, but they liked him anyway. Intellectuals are dependent on politicians to get things done, and conservative intellectuals and columnists claimed to be pleased with what they got.

Did Pres. Ronald Reagan have a "conservative" philosophy? Hardly. He was an attractive spokesman of American clichés about democracy, patriotism, high taxes, and the threat of Communism. He shared the views of the corporate and country-club class, and he had the knack of making them appealing to millions who would never reach that level. He liked to criticize big government, but government continued to grow. His tax cuts fuelled a speculative "boom" based on debt that assisted his reelection, but led eventually to a "bust" with which his successor had to deal. Reagan managed some deregulation, but he was politically shrewd enough to leave most of our sprawling federal government in place. His vast defense expenditures paid off politically in contracts, jobs, and votes. The arms race weakened both countries—the Soviets fatally.

His successor, Pres. George H. Bush, tried to make Reaganism last for one more round, but he lacked the movie-star's show-biz charm and cheerful fiscal irresponsibility. In 1990, faced with rising inflation and interest rates growing out of Reagan's deficits, Bush faced reality and agreed to a budget that raised income taxes and began budget cuts. Bush had committed the ultimate sin: he had destroyed the fantasies of the faithful, and for that he was rejected by many of his own party.

Now we have another Bush in the White House, who seems determined to return to the failed policies of Reaganism: massive tax cuts for the wealthiest Americans, a hurried arms build-up, a foreign policy that is highly unsettling to the global community, a costly war and commitment in Iraq, and deficits as far as the eye can see. The experience of the Reagan years showed that a lasting economic recovery cannot be built on a foundation of public debt. Can this destabilizing and destructive agenda be called "conservative"?

For decades Republican electoral rhetoric identified the Democrats as the party of "big government" and "tax and spend." The Republicans have now become the party of bigger government and "borrow and spend." Conservatism has dwindled to tax cuts without regard to expenditures, militarism without reasonable objectives, under-funding the federal social programs upon which all but the wealthiest Americans rely, and a burden of debt that depresses the economy and the once-mighty American dollar.

A disturbing trend among some Conservative intellectuals is the notion that the United States should exercise an active global hegemony. They propose that the United States cast off the "shackles" of established international institutions and treaties and act unilaterally to bring peace and order to our quarrelsome and disorderly world—presumably for the good of everyone. This idea has some appeal to people who ignore the cost:

super-patriots cheering on the flag, macho types who want to "kick butt," people who turn war into a sporting event, global business interests that think they can follow the troops to a pot of gold, and even some mis-guided Liberals, who are more concerned with correcting problems abroad than creating a better democracy at home.

Few Americans seem at all interested in becoming a twenty-first century version of the Roman Empire. All too often they do not see where the excitement leads until national impoverishment, unemployment, and the decay of public services bring them face to face with the cost of arrogance. Liberals have a responsibility to stand up for common sense when public opinion is seized by one of America's periodic fits of militancy.

The true conservatives are the Liberals, for they wish to maintain, improve, and reform our existing institutions and act positively to deal with the problems that inevitably arise in a dynamic country. The challenge to Liberals is to demonstrate to ordinary Americans that a realistic but forward-looking Liberalism will best conserve the gains of the past and meet the needs of the future.

5

Economic Liberalism

Given good government, the American people will create a prosperous economy. The essentials are clear enough: a strong federal government, abroad and at home; responsible federal finance, including a willingness to tax to meet national needs; a stable currency, and a substantial investment in our infrastructure, environment, and people. These should be the economic principles of Liberals for the foreseeable future.

The Classical Economics

Liberalism has an important economic dimension, but at the outset it must be said that Liberalism never gave primary consideration to *homo economicus*. Liberalism is a philosophy of personal freedom and fulfillment, and the economy is only one consideration. One of the disturbing features of recent years has been the rise of economists, with their narrow vision, to the position of gurus in American public life.

Economic Liberalism rests upon the ideas of Adam Smith as expressed in his *Wealth of Nations* (1776). Smith's masterpiece was an attack on the old economic order, and was as revolutionary as *The Declaration of Independence*. Smith demolished the principles of mercantilism—control of the economy by government, guilds, or official monopolies—and replaced them with an economic model based on private enterprise functioning within a free, competitive market. His successors, David Ricardo and John Stuart Mill refined the model, which still has validity wherever free competitive markets exist.

In the first half of the nineteenth century, Britain made the transition to a free-market, competitive economy and a stable currency based on gold.

During the Victorian hey-day, William E. Gladstone gave the Liberal Party a tradition of sound, economical public finance that was characteristic of nineteenth-century Liberalism. With a policy of low taxes, balanced budgets, free trade, and a stable currency, Britain became the economic leader of the world.

Like the United States after World War II, Britain in the reign of Queen Victoria was so strong economically that the world beat a path to her door. Britain clung to free trade and convertibility of the pound sterling into gold until 1931–32, when the World Depression led Britain to abandon the gold standard and impose a protective tariff. After World War II the British turned to the Labour Party, which introduced a planned economy, national ownership of major industries, trade union power, exchange controls, and a comprehensive welfare state. Although the new system was probably necessary to rebuild Britain's shattered economy, it performed poorly in the dynamic world of the 1960's and the depressed, inflation-wracked world of the 1970s.

The modern heir to the historic policies of Liberalism was Margaret Thatcher, leader of the Conservative Party. Mrs. Thatcher confronted a major economic crisis in 1979 when she became Prime Minister. She cut taxes and spending, privatized socialized industries, deregulated financial markets and foreign exchange, and broke the disruptive powers of the trade unions. She undertook to reform the welfare state, but that was a tough nut to crack. John Major (Conservative) her successor, and Tony Blair (Labour), who succeeded Major as Prime Minister, accepted Thatcherite economic principles, and today Britain is thriving economically.

The French and other continental countries never fully adopted the principles of the Classical Economics. They always preserved a strong role for the state in the economy. Friedrich List's *A National System of Political Economy* (1842) was a neo-mercantilist statement of principles influential in the German states and elsewhere. The continental model is now embodied in the European Union, which has established free trade among its members, offset by a multiplicity of regulations and subsidies, but the EU is protectionist toward the outside world. At present the European Union is prosperous, but stagnant. The dim prospects for economic growth have led to proposals for liberalization, but powerful political and economic interests and labor organizations stand in the way, and substantial change seems unlikely. Addition of new members from Eastern Europe in 2004 further complicates the economic problems of the EU.

The most dramatic triumph of Economic Liberalism in recent years was the attempt to introduce a market economy into Russia after the collapse of the Soviet Union. Even in China, which was the most rigid example of Communist economics, the free economy is making inroads. The East Asian "tigers" are thriving as centers of capitalism, and Chile is a striking example of economic growth based on market principles.

Economic Liberalism in the United States

In the early years of the American republic, the principles of Economic Liberalism, as expounded by Adam Smith and the other Classical Economists, were taken for granted. The only question was the extent to which those principles should be violated in the interest of nation-building, an important objective to a new nation seeking to establish its authority at home and gain respect abroad.

The two main strands in American liberal economic policy appeared in the first year of our republic in the contrasting views of Alexander Hamilton and Thomas Jefferson. Their differences did not concern private enterprise, which has never been seriously challenged in the United States, but the role of the federal government in economic development. Hamilton wanted to use federal powers to encourage banking, commerce, and industry. Hamilton's policies had the potential of producing a kind of neo-mercantilism with a privileged political-economic elite, although in 1791 that elite would have been very small.

True to his egalitarian principles, Jefferson advocated an economy of small businessmen and farmers. He opposed privileges for banking, manufacturing, and trade, and feared the development of a big-business elite that might undermine American democracy. This point of view found a powerful exponent in Pres. Andrew Jackson.

Historical development showed that Hamilton had correctly judged the potential of the United States. The policies he advocated, such as a central bank and tariff protection, contributed to the development of an advanced economy. The Lincoln administration was Hamiltonian, establishing a national banking system and protective tariff, and investing in the economy through the transcontinental railroad, the land-grant colleges, and the Homestead Act.

By the early twentieth century, however, the United States had reached a point where the alliance of big government and big business indicated that Jefferson's fears were not groundless. The Progressive Movement claimed that political and economic freedom were threatened by a new elite of financiers, industrialists, and the railroads. The Progressives (Republicans and Democrats) emphasized reform of government at all levels to root out corruption and privilege. The Sherman Anti-Trust Act, passed by a Republican President and Congress, was intended to preserve competition by breaking up combinations of businesses (trusts) large enough to dominate their markets. Woodrow Wilson, a Democrat, and a Democratic Congress passed the Clayton Anti-Trust Act, which strengthened government regulation of business. The Pure Food and Drug Act and establishment of the Federal Trade Commission were important steps in consumer protection. Liberals believe in economic freedom, but they recognize that modern industrial capitalism requires regulation to prevent abuse of corporate power.

The Progressive impulse resulted in two economic measures that set the direction that Liberalism would take in the twentieth century. One was a constitutional amendment to permit a progressive income tax, which gave the federal government an important new source of revenue and required those who had benefited most from America to pick up more of the cost. Without the income tax, the crucial role of the federal government in modern America would have been impossible.

The other great liberal measure of this period was the establishment of the Federal Reserve System. Its purpose was to give stability to America's hodge-podge of banks, so subject to corruption and panics. Acting as a central bank, the Federal Reserve System supplemented gold and silver with a reliable paper money, giving the nation a flexible money supply and easing the tight money resulting from the gold standard.

The new federal role in the national economy was intended to strengthen, not counteract the principles of Economic Liberalism. Neither the income tax nor the Federal Reserve System was intended to be, as they later became, politically charged instruments for management of the national economy. The federal income tax was for revenue only: it had a low rate and a high level of exemptions, and it did not include "tax breaks" to encourage certain kinds of economic activity. Likewise, the Federal Reserve Board was intended to be politically independent and exercise its powers purely to provide a flexible but stable and reliable currency. America would be well advised to return to those two principles.

Keynesian Economics

For the first century and a half of our country the role of the federal government in the economy was modest, except in time of war. Budgets were balanced most of the time, and money was based on gold and silver supplemented by banknotes. The most important interference of the federal government in the economy was the protective tariff, where strong partisan differences often existed.

Keynesian Economics was introduced into the American economy in response to a national and global disaster—the Great Depression of 1929–1940. Although the Depression began with the collapse in 1929 of a speculative boom on Wall Street, the main factor was a breakdown of world trade and finance that took place between 1929 and 1931. The problem was aggravated by the usual Republican panacea, higher tariffs. Other major industrial countries adopted similar policies to protect their industries and currencies. The breakdown of global markets in money and goods converted a necessary economic adjustment into a World Depression and eventually led to war, as Germany and Japan sought new economic outlets by conquest.

This economic disaster led to the replacement of the Classical Economics by the economics of John Maynard Keynes, a leading figure in the British Liberal Party. Keynes, like Adam Smith, accepted the key role of markets in economic activity, but he advocated government involvement to stimulate and stabilize markets. One tool was fiscal policy, which meant deficit spending by the central government to stimulate the economy in times of depression, to be offset by budget surpluses when the economy recovered. The other was monetary policy. In times of depression (deflation), the central bank would increase the money supply to provide a stimulus; if inflation appeared, excess purchasing power would be reduced by cutting the money supply. Working together, fiscal and monetary policy would keep economic activity at a sustainable level, and thus would check the capitalist tendency toward unwarranted expansion ("boom") and the inevitable contraction ("bust").

Pres. Franklin Delano Roosevelt relied on presidential leadership and the federal government to meet new needs. The Roosevelt administration adopted Keynesian Economics, but in the depressed circumstances of the 1930s, Keynesianism did not work very well. With high unemployment, domestic consumption fell. The breakdown of world trade devastated exports. There was no shortage of money for investment; interest rates were at historic lows. What was lacking was confidence in the long-term future. Nothing would persuade businessmen to invest in capital goods or hire more workers.

The only way to stimulate consumer demand was for the federal government to supply additional purchasing power, which would require deficit spending. Relief payments were provided for the unemployed, and great public works were undertaken. Military expenditures were modestly increased. Federal spending mitigated the effects of the Depression on business and the unemployed, but did not restore confidence or encourage investment. World War II ended the Great Depression. With a guaranteed market, businesses invested in war plants, which provided full employment at good wages. Price controls and rationing kept inflation in check until they were abandoned after the war.

As the war came to a close, American leaders realized that the principal cause of the Depression had been the breakdown of world markets in money and goods. Advised by Keynes, the United States took the lead in establishing the International Monetary Fund and the World Bank to stabilize international exchange and forestall local crises that might bring another general collapse. The dollar became the international medium of exchange and measure of value. The Marshall Plan and other Cold War expenditures helped revive global markets The post-war reconstruction of the world economy was the ultimate triumph of Keynesianism.

Keynesian Economics was the basis for the Kennedy tax cuts in 1963. Under Eisenhower the American economy had been stagnant and unemployment had been high. Walter Heller, a distinguished Keynesian economist, advised Kennedy that a sharp cut in the income tax, combined with increased spending for defense and space that was already in place, would stimulate consumer spending and jump-start the economy into growth. Conditions were ripe for this Keynesian policy, and after the tax cuts the longest economic boom in American history began. The Kennedy tax cuts of the 1960s, when inflation was low and investor confidence was high, became a panacea invoked time and again when economic conditions were entirely different and the consequences were harmful.

In the early 1960s, Americans were filled with confidence and energy, and a splendid generation of "baby boomers" was approaching adulthood. These glowing prospects were destroyed by the enormous costs of pursuing a will o' the wisp in Vietnam. Under Pres. Lyndon Johnson, escalation of the war stimulated a rapidly rising inflation, defense industries crowded out more productive enterprises, and rising interest rates discouraged investment. Despite his lauded diplomatic initiatives to China and the Soviet Union, the core of the Nixon foreign policy was prolongation of the Vietnam War, with the enormous expense and national disruption that the war caused. When inflation threatened his re-election, Nixon imposed wage and price controls that distorted the economy for years. The once-mighty dollar could not sustain its crucial role as the monetary lynchpin of the world economy, and fell precipitously on foreign exchanges. The damaging effects of a misguided and mismanaged war had never been so strikingly displayed.

In the 1970s it became evident that the United States was entering a period of economic difficulty, despite the inherent strength of its government, economy, and people. The world was flooded with dollars spent on foreign policy and war while domestic needs languished. The major oil producers raised oil prices to unprecedented levels. Consequently, vast quantities of dollars flitted through the international money markets, looking for the best return. Global inflation was the inevitable result.

Previously, inflation was supposed to stimulate investment and consumption, as investors and consumers found more money in their pockets. In the new economic conditions, inflation did not stimulate the economy and aggravated unemployment. Businesses found profits falling behind costs, and consumers found prices outstripping wages. The result was an unprecedented economic phenomenon—"stagflation"—which meant a stagnant or declining economy at a time of high inflation. It was clear that the prescriptions of Keynesian Economics did not work in the high-inflation global economy of the 1970s. Obviously a fresh approach was needed.

Milton Friedman and "Monetarism"

An alternative was offered by the "monetarism" of Milton Friedman of the University of Chicago, whose ideas gave a new turn to Liberal Economics. Friedman argued that stagflation was the result of rising interest rates based on inflation and anticipated inflation. Instead of Keynesian monetary and fiscal stimulus, he reversed Keynes and advocated a stable, noninflationary monetary policy that left interest rates, exchange rates, prices, and wages to the ebb and flow of the market. This approach could not work without its essential corollary: balanced federal budgets.

The new Economic Liberalism was based on recognition that the American economy was part of a global market. It was no longer possible to use fiscal and monetary policy to affect the economy of any one country, even a country as strong as the United States. Since much world trade was conducted in dollars, including the international trade in oil, fiscal and monetary restraint by the United States was essential to the health of the world economy.

In October 1979, the Federal Reserve Board, under its new Chairman, Paul Volcker, adopted monetarism and gave priority to a monetarist attack on inflation. As one member of the Federal Reserve Board remarked: "When the party gets good, we take away the punch bowl."

Volcker showed that monetarism could be effective against inflation. He drastically contracted the money supply, leaving the markets scrambling for money to cover their obligations. "Tight money" at first drove interest rates sky-high. With the cost of borrowing at prohibitive levels, the economy spun into the worst recession since 1933. Pres. Jimmy Carter, who deserved better, was the political victim of Volcker's crash program.

Unfortunately, in the 1980s the principles of Volcker and Friedman were violated to accommodate the politics of Reaganism. Pres. Ronald Reagan's budgets were based on tax cuts for the wealthy and large increases in defense spending. Reagan cited the example of the Kennedy tax cuts. Conditions, however, were different, and the result was a fiscal disaster. Sen. Howard Baker, a sensible Republican, called Reaganism "a riverboat gamble," but went along anyway. When David Stockman, Director of the Bureau of the Budget, complained to a journalist that "the numbers don't add up," he was excoriated for criticizing an administration that had discovered the Midas touch. This reckless public finance was called "supply-side economics" by the Reaganites and "voodoo economics" by presidential candidate George H. Bush.

To offset the damaging effects of cuts in the income tax, the Social Security tax, a regressive burden on the productive part of the economy (employers, workers), was increased. Increased payroll taxes were a burden on industry that reduced competitiveness in the world market and contributed to the export of jobs. In short: the goose was taxed to provide golden eggs for the wealthy. The money was spent as it came in, although supposedly it went into a "trust" fund. Recognizing the popularity of Ronald Reagan, Congressional Democrats went along to get the spending needed for the programs that concerned them and their constituencies.

Tax cuts and increased defense spending brought a short-term "boom" that accomplished its purpose—the reelection of Ronald Reagan in 1984. The longer-term result was the inevitable "bust." Banks and S & Ls, especially in the South and West, lent freely on speculative projects. Heavy federal borrowing kept interest rates high and sucked in outside money. The result was a high dollar that injured American exports and put America even more deeply in hock to foreigners. Sensing inflation down the road, investors kept long-term interest rates high. As interest rates rose, businesses stopped investing, plants were shut down, people were laid off, and consumers stopped buying.

The Federal Reserve played along with the politicians by increasing the money supply to fund a tripling of the national debt. The Federal Reserve Board turned out to be, not a group of Platonic philosopher kings who would take away the punch bowl, but tipsy participants in the party. Recession again stalked the land.

In 1990 the administration of Pres. George H. Bush and the Democratic Congress had to face reality: a budget deal was made to raise taxes and cut spending. The Reagan fiscal binge had ended. The Republican right wing never forgave Bush for violating his no-tax pledge, and he left office a disappointed man.

Foreign affairs aggravated the situation. Saddam Hussein, dictator of Iraq, invaded and seized the oil-rich pseudo-country of Kuwait in the Persian Gulf. The Bush administration prepared for war. Oil prices rose at the prospect of war in the Middle East. The airlines were especially hard-hit, since much of the world's supply of aviation gasoline was refined in Kuwait. Travel and tourism, one of the world's major industries, collapsed.

The Bush administration and its allies won a stunning military victory in the Gulf War, but the economic effect of the war aggravated the recession. Saddam Hussein destroyed the oil wells and refining capacity of Kuwait—an economic and ecological disaster. The Bush presidency had its brief moment of triumph, but the recession continued and Bush never regained public confidence. So much for military glory!

When the new Democratic president, Bill Clinton, took office, steps were taken to implement the principles of fiscal and monetary responsibility that were the core of the new Liberal Economics. The budget of 1993 (FY 1994) raised taxes and trimmed spending. Reluctantly the Congressional Democrats concurred, and the budget was passed in the Senate by the casting vote of Vice-President Al Gore. Together, the Bush and Clinton increases brought federal taxes back to the pre-Reagan level. The result was a growing revenue that put federal finances on a sound footing and gave a burst of confidence to businessmen and consumers.

Clinton was a quick learner but a cautious politician. Slowly he brought spending under control and redirected spending priorities. Fiscal responsibility brought investor confidence. The economy began to revive. Investment in America, foreign and domestic, stimulated economic growth and created millions of new jobs. As the economy thrived, unexpected surpluses made possible reduction of the national debt and repayment of debts owed to the Social Security "trust" fund.

When the administration of George W. Bush came into office in January 2001, the first step, for reasons that defied logic and experience, was to abandon the Clinton economic policy, which had worked splendidly. Bush proposed Reagan-sized tax cuts for the wealthy and an increase in defense spending. The Congressional Democrats, craven as always, joined in the party. The predictable result was a recession in 2001 followed by economic stagnation and massive federal deficits.

Consumer spending, which is two-thirds of the economy, continued strong, but employment sagged, as employers shed jobs to remain afloat. Cautioned by the fiscal irresponsibility of the Bush administration, anti-Americanism in the Arab world, volatile oil prices, and the fixation of the American media on terrorism, foreign investment, which had stimulated the Clinton prosperity, slowed to a trickle. The dollar began to slip on international markets. It appeared that the new Liberal Economics, which had brought a short-lived period of fiscal stability and economic growth, had been put on the shelf, while tax cuts, war, and deficits once again shaped the economic policies of the U. S. government.

Liberal Economics for the Future

The most important economic challenges to the United States in the twenty-first century arise from the globalization of economic activity. The flows of people, money, goods, and information throughout the world have created unprecedented economic opportunities and hazards. With responsible leadership, the United States should flourish in the new economic environment.

The global economy of the twenty-first century suggests a fresh look at liberal economics. Liberals should accept the prerequisites of post-Keynesian Liberal Economics: balanced budgets and a stable, non-inflationary money supply. At present the dollar is the global medium of exchange, although some world leaders are beginning to talk of abandoning the dollar for the euro or a basket of currencies. There are some disadvantages to providing the international currency, but the advantages are much greater. To remain the center of international finance and trade in a global world, it is utterly essential to sustain the strength of the dollar, and that can be done only by adopting stable fiscal and monetary policies. This must be an essential element in any liberal agenda.

Liberals should continue the Hamiltonian-Lincolnian-Rooseveltian tradition of a strong federal government that invests in the resources (human and otherwise) of our country. Liberals accept the principle that capitalism must be regulated to protect the health and safety of consumers and prevent abuse of corporate power. Stunning revelations of corporate wrongdoing at Enron and other great corporations have made that principle evident. The long-established principles of the Sherman Anti-Trust Act and subsequent legislation should be used to protect the public interest (which is the national interest) against anti-competitive collusion among businessmen. The Securities and Exchange Commission should be strengthened, to guarantee honest and open markets and prevent accounting rip-offs like the Enron swindle. Adam Smith's distrust of politicians and businessmen, especially when they put their heads together, should be fundamental to all Liberal economic policy.

The advantages of the market economy are great, but the free market is by no means cost free. The global age will require well-educated people who can manage information and fill complex jobs. High-level education of workers must be a national imperative. Just as industrialism required large investments in factories and railways, the information age will require large investments in education and training. Protection of the environment from pollution and preservation of areas of natural beauty from corporate exploitation are essential to providing a good life for all. Public provision (retraining, unemployment benefits) must be provided for people who pay the price of economic growth through unemployment or dislocation. Liberals must make this kind of investment a high priority.

The United States is the essential leader of the globalizing economies of the liberal democracies. Its location between the Atlantic and Pacific economic areas is ideal. Its political system is strong but flexible; its economy is open to talent, enterprise, and innovation; its people are varied but united by common language, laws, and ideals. It is still the land of opportunity, as evidenced by millions of immigrants, most of whom succeed and establish their homes and families here.

In the past forty years, the potential of this great country has been seriously damaged by excesses in foreign policy and war, fiscal irresponsibility, and the capture of the politicians by interest groups seeking favors. The United States cannot thrive in the global economy, nor can it exercise economic leadership, without good government, which at present we do not have. Given good government, the American people will create a prosperous economy. The essentials are clear enough: a strong and active federal government, abroad and at home; responsible federal finance, including a willingness to tax to meet national needs; a stable currency; and a substantial investment in our infrastructure, environment, and people. These should be the economic principles of Liberals for the foreseeable future.

6

Liberalism and Foreign Policy

The essence of Liberal foreign policy is hope; the essence of Conservative foreign policy is fear. Both are mistaken.

Liberal Nationalism and Internationalism

Ever since their origins in the Middle Ages, the main interest of the European states has been foreign policy and war. Determined to make the state a servant of the people, Liberals advocated constitutional and political restraints on their leaders' freedom of action in dealing with other countries, especially where war was a possibility.

Liberal views of the relations among states have had two main strands, which can and should be compatible, but can also be contradictory. One of them is a foreign policy based on Liberal Nationalism, which is primarily concerned with maintaining national sovereignty and securing liberal institutions at home. In Britain, the stout figure of beef-eating, beer-drinking John Bull emerged as a national symbol, displaying defiance of foreign despots behind the wooden walls of the Royal Navy. Liberal Nationalism in American foreign policy was symbolized by Uncle Sam, a tall, lean, sharp-eyed, no nonsense character with a stove-pipe hat and a pointed beard, who stood up for American sovereignty, waggled his bony finger at foreign countries, and, upon occasion, issued to Americans the steely-eyed demand: "Uncle Sam wants YOU!"

The other strand in liberal foreign policy is Liberal Internationalism, which seeks to work within an international community to resolve disputes among states peacefully. In 1795, with war breaking out in Europe, Immanuel Kant, the philosophical culmination of the Age of Reason, published his *Toward Perpetual Peace*. He expected that the same principle that had led people to form states to preserve internal order would lead them to form an international organization to preserve peace among states. Alfred, Lord Tennyson, poet of Victorian aspirations and anxieties, foresaw a time when "the war drums throbbed no longer, and the battle flags were furled/In the Parliament of Man, the Federation of the world."

The Victorians had a difficult time deciding between Liberal Nationalism and Liberal Internationalism. Britain was an island country with a powerful navy and did not fear invasion. As the leading center of finance and industry, Britain did not face foreign economic competition. For almost a century the British followed a policy of Liberal Nationalism most of the time, and they thrived.

There were also good reasons for Britain to support Liberal Internationalism. With her sprawling empire and far-flung trade, Britain depended on peace and open markets. Britain's most important trade was with Europe, where the British saw themselves as the protectors of small states against the aggrandizements of the great powers.

But the Royal Navy exerted power only to the water's edge. Britain had a small army, stationed mainly in the empire, and did not have the military power to intervene actively in European wars. Cooperation with the European states, and later with the United States, was consistent with Britain's liberal ideals, but also with her economic interests and military capabilities.

By the end of the nineteenth century, as nationalism and militarism intensified, many liberal politicians and writers believed that an international organization representing the human community was the best way to settle disputes among nations without resort to war. A spate of international conferences took place. The most influential were the Hague conferences of 1899 and 1907, which created the Hague Tribunal to arbitrate disputes between nations, prepared a code of international law, and advocated systematic efforts at disarmament.

Nevertheless, the powers of Europe sorted themselves out into two heavily armed alliances, each fearful that the other would strike first. Britain abandoned her "glorious isolation" and joined with France and Russia in the Triple Entente. As World War I was breaking out on the continent, a great debate took place within the Liberal government concerning Britain's obligations, if any. When the Liberals saw Germany, "that great bully," attack France through Belgium in August 1914, they took Britain into the fray. In the 1920s, Britain was the country most devoted to internationalism and the League of Nations.

Liberal Nationalism and Internationalism in American Foreign Policy

Throughout the nineteenth century, Liberal Nationalism was dominant in American foreign policy. Americans liked to quote George Washington's warning against "foreign entanglements." The Monroe Doctrine stated American opposition to the extension of European despotism and wars to the Western hemisphere. It also affirmed the determination of Americans to mind their own business in relation to Europe's quarrels, a definition of foreign policy that most Americans found satisfactory for almost a century.

Most of the time foreign policy was a minor concern to Americans. The United States was far from the centers of power in Europe, and Americans built a strong navy to protect their trade and their shores. Otherwise, they were perfectly safe and largely self-sufficient. They maintained a miniscule army, because there was nobody to attack them and they did not intend to become involved in European conflicts.

It was a Liberal, Pres. Woodrow Wilson, who first plunged the United States into the dangerous waters of Liberal Internationalism. In 1917, Wilson took the United States into World War I on the Allied side. At first most Americans, including many Liberals, were dubious about the war, but presidential theatre, patriotic and militaristic hoopla, and "American boys" in combat carried the day.

In his "Fourteen Points," Wilson attempted to convert the war into a crusade for Liberal Internationalism. He advocated extending throughout the world the liberal ideals of democracy and national self-determination. His Liberal Internationalism included a world order based on an international organization and international law. Power politics prevailed, as usual, at the Versailles Peace Conference (1919), but Wilson achieved his principal objective—establishment of the League of Nations.

When the results of World War I were seen, disillusionment was swift, and Americans returned to their historic nationalist foreign policy. They rejected Wilson's League of Nations and declared that they wanted no more involvements in European wars. For a variety of reasons, Americans were not isolationist about Asia. Americans felt strong sympathies for China, and the rise of Japan as a despotic, militaristic, imperialistic power aroused concern. Nor were they isolationist in regard to Latin America. Closer relations with Latin American nations, as in Pres. Franklin D. Roosevelt's "Good Neighbor Policy," were seen as a counter-balance to rising political and economic tensions in Europe and East Asia.

As World War II approached, most American Liberals, including Pres. Roosevelt, favored support for Britain and France and the liberal ideals that those countries represented. Conservatives (mainly Republicans), on the other hand, were almost solidly isolationist. When the threat to peace came from right-wing dictators who claimed to be anti-Communist, American Conservatives were willing to let them go about their bloody business. In any case, the crucial decisions were made by Prime Minister Neville Chamberlain of Britain, supported by the French. Chamberlain attempted to "appease" (satisfy) Hitler by agreeing to his demand for the German-speaking part of Czechoslovakia. Chamberlain had disastrously misjudged the character and ambitions of Hitler. When Hitler revealed his determination to dominate Europe by absorbing the rest of Czechoslovakia and attacking Poland, Britain and France declared war. Too late!

The United States remained neutral when war broke out in Europe in September 1939, although Pres. Roosevelt admitted that he and many Americans were not neutral in spirit. Americans were shocked in 1940 when France collapsed under the assault of the German *Blitzkrieg*. Early in 1941 the Lend-Lease Bill was passed to provide massive American economic and military aid to Britain, then on its last legs due to German bombing and submarine warfare.

The internationalist and nationalist alternatives were thoroughly debated while the Lend-Lease bill was pending. Since that time it has been commonly agreed that the interventionists got the better of the argument, and the isolationists were left to the ignominy that history inflicts on losers. "Appeasement" of dictators was identified as the cardinal sin of foreign policy, often to the extent that the normal give and take of diplomacy became impossible.

The matter was settled when Japan attacked the United States at Pearl Harbor and Hitler recklessly declared war on the United States. At that point, Americans set about winning the war, not disdaining an alliance with the Soviet Union that was unquestionably essential to victory over Germany.

The Cold War: Phase I

During World War II Franklin Roosevelt—Woodrow Wilson's heir in so many ways—established Liberal Internationalism as the governing principle in American foreign policy. Roosevelt believed (rightly) that Europe's long history of bloody wars resulted from balance of power politics, militarism, "spheres of influence," and colonial rivalries. He and his wife, Eleanor, were determined to rectify the conditions that had led to a breakdown of international order in the 1930s by establishing an international organization with full support of the United States. Roosevelt was the leading spirit behind the United Nations, and the American people responded to his Liberal Internationalism. Roosevelt died in April 1945, but Allied victory was assured, and Eleanor Roosevelt became one of the founders of the United Nations Organization.

In addition to the United Nations, the United States entered into many other international institutions and agreements intended to establish a rational, progressive, and peaceful post-war order among the countries of the world. It is fair to say that these institutions have had effects that have been beneficial, although large exceptions must be made for the United Nations, the most idealistic of them all.

The second factor promoting American Liberal Internationalism was the rise of the Soviet Union—a thoroughly totalitarian state—to a great power. When World War II ended, Germany was divided, roughly along the lines occupied by the Allied and Soviet armies. The Soviet Union took control of Eastern Europe through Communist parties backed up by Soviet military force. They actively attempted to advance their influence in Western Europe through Communist parties. Soviet power was strengthened by Communist ideology, for the breakdown of capitalism in the 1930s and the great victories of the Soviet Union in World War II had given Communism a degree of prestige it had not formerly enjoyed.

American Liberals rose to meet the challenge. The energy that had been directed toward the defeat of Germany and Japan was turned toward checking further advances of the new threat to liberal principles of democracy, internationalism, and world peace.

Phase I of the Cold War was led by Pres. Harry Truman. Liberals were the leaders in establishing NATO, the Marshall Plan, and other inter-governmental organizations to check the expansion of Soviet power and Communist ideology. Truman gave Gen. Douglas MacArthur a free hand to establish liberal democracy in Japan.

American foreign policy under Harry Truman was a triumph of American Liberal Internationalism. It was the Democrats who stepped forward to save Western Europe from political and economic collapse, Communist subversion, and possible Soviet invasion. One of the "Great Lies" perpetrated by the Republicans that infected American foreign policy for decades was that the Democrats were "soft on Communism."

Liberalism succeeded in the countries of Western Europe because those countries had the essential pre-conditions of liberal government: experience in self-government, institutions of administration and law with trained people to administer them, an educated population, and advanced economies that supported a substantial middle class. To a considerable extent Japan also possessed the necessary preconditions. MacArthur's "enlightened despotism" transformed Japan into a progressive democracy, and set it on course to become the successful country it is today.

Unfortunately, the American people, knowing little of the world, came to believe that a policy that worked at one place and one time would work anyplace, anytime. The success of NATO and the Marshall Plan in Western Europe and Japan led to recurrent proposals to apply the same principles to parts of the world where the necessary pre-conditions did not exist.

The latest is the idea of spending vast sums to rebuild Iraq into a flourishing democracy.

In the chaos following the defeat of Japan, the Nationalist government of China had fallen to the determined and disciplined Chinese Communists. The Communist victory in China was a blow to those who had hoped that Nationalist China would be a force for peace and stability in the Far East. The second of the "Great Lies" disseminated by the Republicans was that the Democrats "lost China." No one possessed China! China had fallen apart during pre-war revolutionary upheavals and under Japanese occupation. China was taken over by the Communists, who possessed the leadership, unity, determination, and toughness to seize it.

In 1950, Pres. Harry Truman intervened militarily to prevent a takeover of the Korean peninsula by the Communists who ruled the northern part. Gen. Douglas MacArthur had warned against getting involved on the Asian mainland, but something had to be done to show the willingness of the United States to fight, if necessary, to hold the line against the Communist tide. When the Chinese Communists intervened to help the North Koreans, the United States was hard pressed to hold the southern part. The United State paid a heavy price: 50,000 dead and costly financial and military support for South Korea that lasted for decades.

The essence of Liberal foreign policy is hope; the essence of Conservative foreign policy is fear. Both are mistaken. Understandably, many Americans were confused and frightened by the great changes that had taken place in America's world role. The Republicans, desperate to defeat Truman in the presidential election of 1948, took advantage of those people to foment "the Great Fear" that agitated Americans from 1948 to 1952 and after.

Although the United States was far and away the most powerful and safest country in the world, and Communism had virtually no appeal in the United States, the Republicans, led by Sen. Joe McCarthy of Wisconsin, launched an anti-Communist witch-hunt. McCarthy used his senatorial immunity to bring slanderous charges against the heroes of the Cold War: Pres. Truman, Secretaries of State George Marshall and Dean Acheson, and lesser figures who had acted boldly to stop the advance of the Soviet Union and Communism. In so doing, McCarthy made his name a by-word for irresponsible demagogy, but he sounded themes that were widely accepted and reverberated for years after.

In 1953, Pres. Dwight D. Eisenhower made peace in Korea. For all practical purposes the Cold War was over. America had won. The threat of Soviet power and Communist parties to Western Europe and Japan had been stopped. Economic recovery was beginning. It was clear that, if the United States stayed the course, Liberal democracy would prevail in those important parts of the world. The universal ideals of Wilson and Roosevelt had not been fulfilled, but the heartlands of Western Civilization had been saved for Liberal Democracy and were united under American leadership. Realistically, that was the most that could be expected. Unfortunately, Liberals thought that liberal principles could be extended to countries without the necessary pre-conditions, and therein lay the great mistakes of Liberal Internationalism.

The Cold War: Phase II

At the end of World War II it became evident that the Soviet Union had no intention of participating positively in international organizations. Before the war, the Soviet Union had been an outcaste state. Their victories in the war had given the Soviets a taste for the Great Power role, and had encouraged Communist movements throughout the world. As Communists, the Soviets believed that capitalist countries were out to destroy them. This mentality did not change when they became a great military power. Added to that was their belief that Communism was the wave of the future and the Soviet Union was the vanguard.

When the Cold War began under Pres. Truman, it was hoped that a policy of "containment" would eventually bring the Soviet Union to its senses and a peaceful settlement of differences could take place. These hopes were disappointed, and Americans made a gradual transition from Liberal Internationalism to "Militant Internationalism." The United States and the Soviet Union formed powerful military alliances backed up by a frightening new development: nuclear weapons. The world had morphed back to the situation that Wilson had denounced and Roosevelt had tried to prevent: balance of power politics, militarism, "spheres of influence," and rivalries in the unstable nations emerging from colonial status.

Phase II of the Cold War took place in the new zone of instability called "the Third World." These former colonies were of little consequence in the global balance of power, and certainly no threat to the United States or the Soviet Union. Many had recently gained their independence; they needed positive encouragement, but they had to find their own way and live with their mistakes. Absent the controlling hand of the imperial power, and lacking the pre-conditions for Liberal Democracy, territorial, linguistic, tribal and religious conflicts broke out. In some, the army established a military dictatorship that maintained order, usually by brutal means. In others, Communist parties, with similar ruthlessness, established party dictatorships where the party ran things. Americans, who naively thought all peoples wanted political and civil rights, looked on, appalled, and blamed the colonial powers for not preparing their people adequately for independence.

The Communist states looked to the Soviet Union for support and received it as a way to counterbalance the power of the United States. The United States, fired by indiscriminate zeal to block Communist expansion, rushed to the support of right-wing military dictatorships. In this way, the two superpowers entered into a contest for control of immature countries that could mean nothing but trouble and expense for both of them. Through a series of imprudent treaties with Third World dictators and other professed anti-Communist leaders, Republican Cold Warriors led by Pres. Eisenhower's Secretary of State, John Foster Dulles, laid the groundwork for the extension of American Cold War concerns to areas of maximum trouble and minimal strategic or economic importance.

When Ho Chi Minh, a long-established fighter for Vietnamese independence and a professed Communist, seized power in the northern part of Vietnam, the Eisenhower administration forestalled him by establishing an American satellite government in the southern part. Once again, the United States had accepted a costly and dangerous foothold on the landmass of Asia. The American people had paid a heavy price in Korea, and they would eventually pay an even heavier price in Vietnam.

As the Cold War settled in, some Liberals developed a concept of Realistic Internationalism, which took a broad view of America's global role while recognizing the limitations of American power and the unreadiness of many countries and people to accept American ideas. They held that democracy must advance by its own inherent merit, not by American interventions in the politics of other countries, arming and subsidizing political allies, invading to depose dictators, or intervening in insurgencies and civil wars. They knew that a democracy that seeks world leadership must be strong at home. As the principal exemplar and custodian of the democratic ideal, the United States should look first at its own performance. Ignorance, poverty, crime, and racism in the United States weakened the democratic message that America offered to the rest of the world.

When John F. Kennedy was inaugurated in 1961, American Liberals were thrilled by the accession to power of a new generation. Kennedy, scion of a nouveau riche Boston family, was young, handsome, eloquent, witty, and ambitious. Some Liberals [including the author of this book] believed that Kennedy would adopt a policy of Realistic Internationalism that would resolve some of the tensions of the Cold War and enable him to deal with pressing domestic issues such as economic growth, civil rights, and poverty. Why elect a president of a new generation and a different political party just to prolong the Cold War policies of John Foster Dulles?

It turned out that Kennedy's call for America to dedicate itself to "pay any price…to assure the survival and success of liberty" meant intensification of Cold War militancy. By the end of his first year Kennedy had sent the first American military advisers to South Vietnam. The next year his administration engaged in "regime change" by conniving in the assassination of the South Vietnamese leader, Diem. Having done so, America was stuck with creating a new political structure in South Vietnam. When Kennedy was assassinated in 1963, some 14,000 American troops had been sent to support the new government. Vice-President Lyndon B. Johnson, Kennedy's successor, escalated American forces to 500,000 men, but victory eluded him. A broken man, he did not run for reelection in 1968.

The Vietnam War was a grotesque distortion of Liberal Internationalism. No conceivable American national interest was at stake nor was world peace threatened, regardless of which side won. American military forces, built to fight in Europe, were injected into a situation for which they were totally unprepared. Poorly trained draftees were sent to fight an enemy who was familiar with the terrain and climate. The offspring of the middle class (like Bill Clinton, George W. Bush, and Dick Cheney) took refuge in college deferments or the safety of the National Guard, while the kid who worked in the gas station was drafted and sent to a living hell.

American Conservatives, swayed by visceral anti-Communism and the desire to frustrate the domestic agendas of liberal presidents, enthusiastically supported that terrible self-inflicted wound. Tribalism, never far from the surface in American life, erupted—flags, drums, and trumpets were flourished and opponents of the war were damned as "Commies" and "wimps." The misuse of American Nationalism to defend a bad cause confirmed Samuel Johnson's remark: "Patriotism is the last refuge of scoundrels."

At the riotous Democratic national convention in 1968, the Democrats nominated Vice-President Hubert Humphrey, the voice of Liberalism since his early career in Minnesota. Intimidated by Johnson and other Democratic Cold Warriors, Humphrey would not denounce the Vietnam War. Had Humphrey done so, the issue of the war would have been debated in the convention, not in the streets, and he probably would have been elected. Instead, Humphrey handed the peace issue to the shifty Richard Nixon, who said that he had a "secret" plan to end the war. The American people were desperate for peace, and Nixon won the election.

Nixon began a slow withdrawal of American ground troops, but continued the war by bombing, a cruel and ineffective method of fighting in a country with a peasant economy. His clever foreign policy advisor, Henry Kissinger, engaged in protracted peace negotiations intended to cover up the fact that America was losing. Eventually, Congress sneaked out of Vietnam without admitting defeat by refusing to fund the war.

The Vietnam War split the Liberals, since many Liberals [including the author of this book] became outspoken opponents of the war. The Cold

War Liberals were confronted with defending a case that could not be defended. The anti-war Liberals had logic on their side, but powerful interests and strong public feeling against them. The American people saw the war, not as an instrument of foreign policy, but as a contest they were determined to win. The split weakened American Liberalism to a degree that the liberal thrust that had shaped twentieth-century America could never be regained.

The End of the Cold War

Forty years too late, the Cold War finally ended, prolonged by the stubbornness of two superpowers that had trapped themselves in political posturing, heated rhetoric, Cold War economic interests, and a costly and dangerous arms race. America's wealth and technological superiority took American military technology to a level that the Soviet Union could not match. The frantic efforts of the Soviet Union to keep up brought its economy to the point of collapse. Soviet leader Mikhail Gorbachev introduced reforms in a desperate effort to revive the failing Soviet system. Instead, the Soviet Union imploded, and Gorbachev was left holding an empty bag. The satellite states of Eastern Europe overthrew their Communist governments and reclaimed their independence. Russia asserted itself as an independent, sovereign state, and the other republics of the Soviet Union did likewise. In 1990 Germany was re-unified. The Cold War was over, without a shot being fired!

It is wrong to claim that the United States "won" Phase II of the Cold War. Both countries paid a high price for that prolonged war of attrition. The Soviets destroyed their country and we inflicted great damage on our own. America is a strong country and bounced back, but the lost opportunities of those thirty years can never be reclaimed. The weapons that were brought into the Third World countries continue to kill and maim to this day. If the United States was the victor, our victory was like that of the Greek general Pyrrhus, who prevailed in several costly battles against the stubborn Romans. "One more victory like these," Pyrrhus said, "and I am undone."

Militant Internationalism and the Zones of Instability

The collapse of the Soviet Union left the United States as the unchallenged economic and military leader of the world. Americans accepted major responsibility for supporting international institutions and restoring order in the zones of instability that previously had been locked into the superpower rivalries of the Cold War. One area of potential trouble was Eastern Europe, which had been an area of territorial and ethnic conflict for centuries and the place where the two world wars had originated. These countries were devastated and demoralized by forty years of Communist rule, and had no desire to return to the conflicts of the past. They were eager to join economically with Western Europe, and they looked to NATO and the United States for protection against any revival of German or Russian expansion. Germany undertook a costly process of rebuilding the former East Germany, and the European Union began steps to integrate the two halves of Europe economically. Under Pres. Bill Clinton, the NATO shield was extended to Eastern Europe. This process, and the hopes it fostered, stabilized a possible area of war and civil strife. Europe is an area of enormous importance to the United States and the global economy. Clinton's positive steps in Eastern Europe were an appropriate use of American power and influence.

Another dangerous zone of instability was the explosive Middle East, which was especially important as the world's most important source of oil. In 1990 Saddam Hussein, the brutal dictator of Iraq, suddenly invaded the neighboring mini-state of Kuwait, a major oil producer. Pres. George H. Bush, a member of the World War II generation, immediately invoked the memory of Hitler and the failure of "appeasement," and called for military action to stop the aggressor. With the support of the United Nations, Bush led a coalition that assembled a huge military force in the Gulf and liberated Kuwait. Americans cheered as a World War II style offensive rolled over a Third World army that collapsed. The core of Saddam's army escaped and was used by him to suppress uprisings by the Kurdish minority in the north and the Shi'ite Moslems in the south.

Bush refused to invade Iraq and overthrow Saddam, since that was not included in the U. N. mandate. Furthermore, Bush and his Secretary of

State, James Baker, recognized the difficulties and costs of attempting "regime change" in a deeply divided Moslem country. Considering the issues at stake, and the quick military victory, Bush's intervention in Kuwait was justifiable, although the damage done to Iraq by the bombing and the subsequent economic sanctions was great. When Saddam attempted to deter another such attack by developing nuclear and biological weapons, Bill Clinton and Tony Blair responded by bombing suspected weapons sites. This intervention seems to have been sufficient to stop those programs in their tracks, as U. N. inspectors discovered later. The Iraq policies of Bush and Clinton demonstrated that an intervention of limited scope with international support could stabilize a dangerous situation in that important part of the world.

Liberal Internationalism and Human Rights

Fundamental to American Liberalism is the concept of human rights, defined in the *Declaration of Independence* as "life, liberty, and the pursuit of happiness." The Declaration held that "all men" were entitled to these rights, an expression that has been expanded by logical extension to mean all people regardless of nationality, gender, age, race, creed, or social class. As World War II came to a close, the *Charter of the United Nations Organization* proclaimed as one of its purposes "to reaffirm faith in fundamental human rights, in the dignity and worth of the human person, in the equal rights of men and women and of nations large and small." Since that time concern for human rights has been an essential part of American Liberalism, and Liberals have made it an important element in American foreign policy.

With the Cold War, Conservatives also became internationalists as part of their global crusade against Communism. They proclaimed their abhorrence of human rights abuses in Communist regimes, although they were ready to support the human rights abuses of dictatorships of the right. The list of right-wing dictators that the United States has supported in pursuit of its Cold War aims is long: among them were Mobutu in the Congo, Pinochet in Chile, Ramos in the Philippines, Saddam Hussein in Iraq, and Noriega in Panama.

In respect of human rights, a strong dose of Liberal Realism is necessary. Americans engage in demagoguery and self-deception when they proclaim goals that are incapable of fulfillment. Many countries do not have a tradition of human rights or a culture that respects human rights. This is a diverse and badly flawed world by American democratic standards. There are some things that we can do to make it better. Playing the role of global policemen, paymaster, schoolmaster, and scold is not one of them. Our most useful contribution to human rights in other parts of the world is to give a good example at home.

Liberal Realism in International Relations

When World War II and the Cold War thrust the United States into a global role, Americans lacked a clear concept of foreign policy. They had little grasp of the reality that foreign policy is concerned with the relationships among sovereign states, with the purpose of resolving differences peacefully but including the use of force, if necessary. In the 1930s, isolationists had claimed that the United States could ignore unwelcome developments in other parts of the world. After World War II, isolationism was replaced by an interventionist mentality that said the United States could NOT ignore unwelcome developments in any part of the world. To draw distinctions between different peoples based on power, culture, and the national interest was seem as an invidious violation of American universalism.

Liberals were true to American ideals when they declared that the best way to extend democracy and freedom was to make the United States a shining example to the rest of the world. They showed good judgment when they committed American military power and economic resources to the defense and recovery of Western Europe and Japan. Liberals lost their way, however, when they proclaimed their commitment to democracy in countries that totally lacked the pre-conditions of a liberal-democratic government or society. They overlooked the great differences created by language, history, level of economic development, education, religion, and culture among the many and diverse peoples of the world. Anything less than concern for all mankind was condemned as selfishness, isolationism,

Eurocentrism, or racism—attitudes damned forever by the evil example of Hitler.

It is time for a reorientation of American foreign policy, and—as always—Liberals must take the lead. The first place to begin is to return to the principles embodied in our constitution. With the conduct of European kings in mind, our founding fathers were well aware of the fatal attraction of foreign policy and war to those who hold power in the state. They required Senate consent to treaties, and they looked to the power of the purse to enable both houses to check an overly ambitious president.

They did not anticipate an extended network of executive agreements that evaded the treaty clause, a Senate that would collude with the executive branch in its over-weening ambitions, nor a Congress that would be a partner with presidents in costly ventures overseas. They did not anticipate a swollen Defense Department whose large expenditures would become an important consideration in Congress and elections. Of course, adherence to our constitution will not take place if our voters regard foreign policy and war as exciting "reality TV" until the bills and flag-draped coffins come home.

Liberals must step forward and end the fifty-year domination of American public affairs by foreign policy and war, generated by unrealistic hopes and fears and fueled by heedless "war fever" and media sensationalism. The generation that adopted the role of a world power justified its policies by invoking the mistakes of the isolationist generation of the 1930s. So they went to the other extreme. The isolationist generation failed us in important respects, but so did the internationalist generation.

The Liberal message for the twenty-first century must include an American foreign policy based on cool, realistic judgments, not exaggerated, media-driven, vote-seeking reactions to threats, real or imaginary. Nor can it be a crude, unilateral exercise of power without consideration of our national interest in a peaceful world of nations that work together.

The United States should and inevitably will be a force in the world, due to its large and energetic population, powerful economy, and leadership in finance, trade, communications, science, technology, and popular culture. We are now a global people, and there are many ways that we can strengthen the emerging world community.

But we should recognize that we do not need to and do not want to be a Great Power in the conventional sense: throwing our weight around, intervening in boundary disputes or civil wars, engaging in embargoes and other forms of economic warfare, making knee-jerk responses to the latest TV crisis, threatening other countries with massive military forces, and occasionally clobbering a patsy like Lebanon, Grenada, Panama, Libya, Afghanistan or Iraq to show that we mean business. If America breaks down under the burdens of foreign policy, militarism, and war—as the Soviet Union did—the great beacon of Liberal Democracy and the lynch-pin of the global economy will have fallen, and a time of troubles will surely follow. As Pogo, the modest little 'possum said: "We have met the enemy, and he is us."

7

Liberalism and War

*Liberals, if they have the courage of their convictions, will insist that any use of force have a serious and necessary purpose, have international support, and be conducted according to humane rules of war. Americans should take up arms only when prepared to follow the example of the **Declaration of Independence** and show "a decent respect to the opinions of mankind."*

Liberalism and the Rules of War

The founders of Liberalism knew about war. The eighteenth century was an age of power politics and periodic conflicts for thrones, territories, and colonies. The thinkers and writers of the Age of Reason did not expect that war would disappear. But they thought that reasonable men could remove its worst excesses.

In Voltaire's satirical novel, *Candide*, the hero's youthful optimism was modified by experience, from which he learned that at its best this world was not very good and at its worst it was very bad indeed. "Everywhere the weak loathe the powerful before whom they cower," Candide's friend pointed out, "and the powerful treat them like flocks of sheep whose wool and flesh are to be sold. A million drilled assassins go from one end of Europe to the other murdering and robbing with discipline in order to earn their bread, because there is no honester occupation."

Jonathan Swift was equally blunt in *Gulliver's Travels*, a cutting satire that tells of the voyages of a typical Englishman, Lemuel Gulliver. On his second voyage, Gulliver found himself shipwrecked in Brobdingnag, a land of huge people who were reasonable and kind. In such company Gulliver was a pipsqueak, and he attempted to magnify himself by boasting about his country. Gulliver was proud of England's prowess in war, especially the havoc wreaked by gunpowder. He attempted to ingratiate himself with the king by revealing the secret of its manufacture.

The king was horrified that Gulliver could appear to be "wholly unmoved at all the scenes of blood and desolation that [he] had painted as the common effects of those destructive machines, whereof [the king] said, some evil genius, enemy to mankind, must have been the first contriver." After hearing Gulliver's report of the history, government, and wars of England, the king concluded that the English must be "the most pernicious race of little odious vermin that nature ever suffered to crawl upon the surface of the earth."

Since war seemed to be endemic to the human condition, liberal thinkers attempted to bring it under reasonable and humane control. In 1625 Hugo Grotius, a Dutchman, published *Concerning the Law of War and Peace*, a seminal treatise on international law. In addition to considering the causes for which war might justly be waged, he gave considerable attention to humane practices for the combatants and for the civilians involved indirectly. Immanuel Kant argued that the self-interest of states would eventually teach them the futility of war. Even a race of intelligent devils, he added, would be smart enough to avoid it.

In the meantime certain principles emerged to civilize war. One step was to establish formal procedures to declare it. Rulers would be required to justify their decision before, not after the fighting began. The authors of our constitution, who were highly civilized men, hedged the war-making power with constitutional provisions requiring a formal declaration of war by Congress.

A second step in civilizing war was to confine it to men under discipline and in uniform. Military discipline restrained the passions of men inflamed by combat. The uniform limited combat to persons who were clearly identifiable and could be held responsible for their conduct. Regulations were also introduced for the humane treatment of prisoners and the wounded. Procedures under military justice were established to punish those who violated the rules.

Disciplined, uniformed armies brought with them another civilizing principle: respect for non-combatants. Although war inevitably ravaged the battlefield and the surrounding area, it was commonly agreed that living off the land and plundering the civilian population without compensation were not to take place.

Finally, the wars of the eighteenth century were not conceived as life and death struggles of the virtuous against infidels. Wars were devoted to the achievement of political objectives, and it was expected that negotiations and fighting would proceed simultaneously, in the hope of a settlement to which all parties could agree.

The Napoleonic Wars, and the century of smaller wars that followed, stimulated thought on the question of war. While conservative thinkers expatiated on the nobility of war as a school of manly virtues, the necessity of the strong to dominate the weak, and the civilizing mission of Western imperialism, liberal thinkers sought ways to tame the beast. The rules of war were refined in the Hague Conferences (1899, 1907) and the Geneva Conventions (1906, 1929). Of course, those rules were often violated, but they expressed the liberal view of war at the beginning of the twentieth century.

World War I was the first war of mass armies against mass armies, populations against populations, and industrial production against industrial production. The destruction of life and property went far beyond all previous wars, as the belligerents marshaled all their resources for "victory" rather than a negotiated settlement. Nevertheless, on the Western Front the established rules of war were generally adhered to, and there was little loss of life or destruction beyond the battlefield itself. The main loss of civilian life came at the end of the war, with revolution, starvation, and epidemics of influenza and diphtheria.

On the battlefield, World War II in Europe was much like World War I, with the exception of the greater mobility and striking power provided by tanks and planes. The rules of war concerning combatants were adhered to reasonably well on the Western Front, but on the Eastern Front there were no rules.

The great difference was the war against civilian populations. World War II was the first modern war in which more civilians died than uniformed soldiers. In World War II, the Germans and Japanese attacked without warning and brutalized the populations that they conquered. Hitler tried to defeat Britain by bombing, but failed. The bombing only made the British people more determined to fight on.

The British and Americans invested enormous resources in strategic bombing, on the assumption (erroneous, as it turned out) that bombing population centers and industry would reduce or even eliminate the need for ground warfare. Recognizing the inaccuracy of high-altitude bombing, the British bombed cities to destroy German morale. The Americans, giving lip service to the rules of war, bombed factories and transportation centers, but since these were almost always located in cities, the effect was the same. Nevertheless, the German Army and people continued fighting to the end.

The fire bombing of Japanese cities was much more destructive of life and property than the two atom bombs. Despite that, the Japanese people had plenty of weapons for home defense and were ready to fight to the bitter end until the atom bombs shocked the Emperor into surrender.

The *Strategic Bombing Survey* at the end of the war found that the effects of bombing on the outcome of the war were modest. Looking back upon his role in the *Survey*, John Kenneth Galbraith summarized the American view as "we have bombers; therefore they are effective." It seems that nothing can shake the American confidence in bombing, despite the loss of life and property inflicted on people with whom we expect to make peace eventually. Bombing people is not a good way to "win hearts and minds."

On the other hand, tactical airpower (fighter planes used in support of ground troops) was exceptionally important in World War II. In the Battle of the Bulge, the German counter-offensive was successful due to cloudy weather. When the skies cleared and American fighter planes came into action, the Germans were doomed.

A major objective of Liberals should be to formulate new rules of war for the twenty-first century. The destructive capability of modern weapons has given military forces unprecedented potential for frightfulness. The nihilistic notion that "war is hell" and therefore "anything goes" must be resisted as destructive of civilization itself.

As a country founded on liberal principles, and boasting the world's largest, best-trained, and best-equipped military forces the United States should take the lead in establishing rules of war that recognize the changed nature of warfare. Consideration should be given to reasonable and humane rules concerning the use of the massive firepower of armored ground forces, cluster bombs and shells, satellite-guided planes and missiles, and nuclear warheads of any size. Military involvements in civil wars, guerrilla war, and counter-terrorism are likely to do more harm than good. Most important of all will be to formulate new rules relative to bombing of cities and the impact of war on civilians.

Liberals, if they have the courage of their convictions, will insist that any use of force have a serious and necessary purpose, have international support, and be conducted according to humane rules of war. Americans should take up arms only when prepared to follow the example of the *Declaration of Independence* and show "a decent respect to the opinions of mankind."

American Liberalism and War

From the beginning, Americans accepted the principle that war, being an evil, should not be used except to forward a cause that is morally good and achievable by the use of military force. The American colonists regarded the Revolution as a defense of their legal and human rights, and an assertion of their potential for nationhood. The *Declaration of Independence* stated in considerable detail the reasons why they had taken up arms against their Mother Country. Abraham Lincoln put the Civil War on a moral footing when he proclaimed the need to preserve the Union and abolish slavery. The *Gettysburg Address* said it all.

Pres. Woodrow Wilson gave World War I a moral purpose as a crusade for democracy, national determination, international law, and a "war to end wars." Americans were bitterly disillusioned when the outcome of the war belied the high moral purposes that Wilson had proclaimed. In World

War II, Pres. Roosevelt and Prime Minister Churchill adopted the universalism of Wilson when they defined the goals of the Allies as the Four Freedoms: freedom of speech and religion, freedom from want, and freedom from fear. Germany and Japan, by their own brutality, provided all the moral justification that the Allies needed. Americans have never doubted that World War II was necessary and just, despite the terrible ravages that took place during that titanic conflict.

With the Cold War, the political trumpet again sounded the cause of Freedom vs. Dictatorship. The NATO alliance and nuclear deterrence worked, and Phase I of the Cold War restored Liberal Democracy to Western Europe and Japan. In Phase II, the Cold War degenerated into a sleazy contest of corruption or subversion of governments in weak, unstable countries, the spread of weapons in places where they were likely to be misused, and an amassing of nuclear overkill that was the most frightening aspect of all. The superpowers sustained huge conventional forces at great expense, although these forces were rarely used. When they were used, as by the Americans in Vietnam or the Soviets in Afghanistan, the result was disaster. In the process, the Soviet Union destroyed itself, and the United States diminished the bright prospects of a generation.

The end of the Cold War afforded a breathing space to reconsider America's role in the world and the rationale for its military forces. Regrettably, that period was not well used. It appears that American militarism, deeply embedded in our national institutions, budget, economy, and psyche has turned toward the Middle East and wars against "rogue states." We should realize that interventions in the conflicts of other countries often make things worse and can spin out of control. War is a poor way to settle most of the problems that we are likely to face.

The President and Congress should expect to pay for a war (or a large part of it) through an increase in taxes; the notion that war can be waged without paying for it is an inducement to ill-considered military involvements. The Vietnam War would probably not have been fought if the great American middle class had been called upon to pay for it through taxes, and had not been given college deferments for its offspring. The bad idea of fighting wars on the cuff has been followed ever since. Even worse is the Bush policy of fighting a war and cutting taxes at the same time.

Americans should keep civilians out of the mayhem as much as possible. Ever since World War II, Americans have regarded bombing as the preferred method for the use of force despite the fallacy of "pin-point bombing" and "surgical strikes". Bombing civilian populations becomes a way of expressing frustration, or taking vengeance on innocent civilians for the sins of their leaders. As we consider the role of war in a democracy, we should reconsider our reliance on such an undiscriminating weapon with its inevitable effects upon civilian populations.

Economic sanctions are a favorite American substitute when our leaders and people are not ready for outright war. Sanctions are a pathetic substitute for a firm foreign policy and almost always fail. Castro continues in power in Cuba while the Cuban people feel the effects of American sanctions. Fourteen years of sanctions did not overthrow Saddam Hussein, but left the economy of Iraq in shambles and imposed useless deprivation on the people.

Liberalism has always rested on a sense of personal and public morality. The failure of Liberals to develop moral principles to control modern war—and to stand up against the debasement of that moral sense due to TV politics and the public's lust for explosions—is symptomatic of American Liberalism's decline.

American Military Forces

Serious consideration must be given to the kind of military forces and personnel that we need in the twenty-first century. The decisiveness of victory in World War II and the moral necessity to fight it have shaped American thinking about war ever since. It is time to ask whether the model of World War II continues to have value fifty years later.

World War II was won with armored ground forces, carrier task forces, and fleets of bombers. These were the armaments maintained by the United States during the forty years of the Cold War, although it became increasingly obvious that they would never be used in a major war. At the end of World War II, the Germans had the ballistic missile and the Americans had the nuclear warhead. Shortly after the war the two were joined, and nuclear ballistic missiles became part of the post-war arsenal. It is arguable that nuclear missiles prevented the land war that many observers expected, but even so, the size, number, and destructive power of those missiles was excessive. The vast nuclear arsenals of the United States and the Soviet Union, with their capacity to destroy civilized life many times, over fully warranted the scornful reaction of the king of Brobdingnag to Gulliver's offer of the secret of gunpowder.

When World War II ended, Americans wanted to demobilize as quickly as possible and get back to their normal lives. The Cold War began the militarization of America. Phase I of the Cold War required large standing forces to contain the Soviet Union and give a sense of security to Western Europe. Phase II of the Cold War was dominated by military interventions in Third World countries. The Defense Department created a structure of bases throughout the world, and made vast contracts that had enormous political clout in Congress and were an important influence on the economy. The abandonment of the draft created a military profession that enjoyed great respect among the people. The word "war" was debased into the expression "the war on (inflation, drugs, AIDS, terrorism)," which was used for almost any effort to eliminate a problem. The existence of large military forces created a temptation to use them, often in places where they could not be effective. And the collapse of the Soviet Union left the United States with unrivalled military power.

As the only military superpower in the world, the United States must rethink the model of World War II and develop military forces suitable to a world far removed from 1945. Do we need heavily armored ground forces, carrier task forces, fleets of bombers, and thousands of nuclear missiles in the emerging world community of the twenty-first century? If not, what kind of military forces do we need?

The United States must maintain the kind of military forces that are needed to achieve national goals and maintain world peace. Clearly, these goals include maintenance of the growing world system of democracy, capitalism, global communications, and freedom of the seas and air. Our forces must be recruited and trained to use modern hi-tech weapons and equipment. They must be light, flexible, quickly deployed, highly mobile, and capable of fighting in difficult environments with minimal supply services. We must be strong in space, which is the high ground that every general wants to hold.

The U. S. Army is still a road-bound, heavily armored force based on awesome firepower. It is designed to fight other armies on an open battlefield. After Vietnam, the Army was determined to avoid involvement in civil and ethnic conflicts on inhospitable terrain. As Chief of Staff, Gen. Colin Powell developed a doctrine that the Army should fight only with overwhelming force and with a clear exit strategy. The Gulf War under the first Pres. Bush met those criteria, and was successful. Now, as Secretary of State under the second Pres. Bush, Powell sees the serious consequences of violating the criteria that he had defined.

Americans must consider our needs for military manpower. Historically, the liberal principle was "the citizen soldier," a principle that served this country well from the American Revolution and the Civil War to World Wars I and II. After the failure in Vietnam, we changed to well-trained forces of men and women who enlisted and were expected to remain in the service for long periods of time. Americans have always regarded these professional military people as citizen soldiers, which they certainly are. The new approach to military manpower seems to work reasonably well. Liberals should insist on personnel policies (pay, benefits, housing, etc.) that make our military services attractive to people of high caliber.

Everyone knows that our ground forces are too small for the missions that we have chosen to undertake. Congress prefers to spend money on procurement, which means contracts, profits, jobs and votes. Expenditures for personnel have little political payoff. That is why the Navy and Air Force receive large contracts for ships and planes, but we do not have enough Army personnel and of the right kind.

The reluctance of Congress to maintain adequate numbers of personnel has led to the misuse of the Reserves, which are intended for short-term emergencies. The National Guard has been diverted from its purpose as a force to control internal disturbances or respond to natural disasters, and now is used for long-term overseas assignments. The men and women of the Reserves and the National Guard have jobs, families, and other commitments. This abuse of their willingness to serve will, in the long run, destroy the system, which still preserves the American concept of "the citizen soldier." Since employers are required to keep their jobs open, long deployments place another burden on American business.

Our regular forces are grossly misused. Their purpose is to use firepower to achieve military objectives in war against the armed forces of another sovereign state. They should not be expected to perform services other than those for which they have been recruited and trained. They should not be sent into a scene of war with orders not to fight. They should not be expected to be peacekeepers, social workers, or distributors of disaster relief. They should not be placed in exposed positions surrounded by a hostile population in a culture that they do not understand. These are the circumstances that they now face in Iraq.

Terrorism

One of the great fallacies of our time is that military forces can be used effectively against terrorism. Terrorists mingle among the civilian population or locate in remote places, and rarely offer targets that military forces can attack. Attempts to do so are likely to generate more terrorists. To claim that the war in Iraq was part of a "war against terrorism" was grossly misleading. Now the war has intensified the threat that it was intended to eliminate. The security of the United States and the stability of the world community are weakened by such a reckless use of military force in such an inflammable part of the world.

Is terrorism war? The word "war" should be limited to conflicts between the armed forces of sovereign states. Ordinary terrorism is not war; it is a crime, and should be dealt with as such. However, terrorism has now reached a level of intensity that is not ordinary. In some parts of the world it is approaching a popular movement. Terrorism has become something that is neither war, in the conventional sense, nor the small-scale terrorist gangs of the past.

Major international efforts will be needed to check the ravages of terrorism, although, as with the effort to control the supply of narcotics, there will probably be no final victory. The first step is to defend against it. Terrorism has to be dealt with by intelligence services, undercover police work, and security measures to protect conspicuous buildings, travelers, military installations, and the like. This kind of work, by its very nature, does not get on television, and hence its political support is weak. Organized terrorist camps in remote places, like those of Osama Bin Laden in Afghanistan, can be broken up by armed force, although the terrorists will scatter to new locations where they will continue their efforts. Other countries fear terrorism as much as we do, and they will work with us in this effort.

The second—and more important—step is to resolve the grievances that cause terrorism. Terrorism is a response of the weak to abuse of power (or perceived abuse of power) by the strong. The basis of Arab terrorism is the Israeli-Palestinian conflict. As the principal supporter of Israel, the United States has a responsibility to use its influence to help resolve this problem.

The oil of the Middle East is important to the world economy, and it is essential to maintain a reliable supply. Western military interventions in the area in the Middle East evoke powerful nationalist and religious reactions. The major advanced countries and oil companies must give the governments and peoples of the Middle East reasons to be participants and sharers in this important resource. Their sovereignty and dignity must be respected. This is an approach that Liberals should support.

8

Social Liberalism

Liberals argued that freedom must mean more than Anatole France's wry defi-
nition: "the equal freedom of the rich and the poor to sleep under bridges."
They decided that personal freedom and dignity in an industrial society
required a decent standard of living for all.

The Roots of Social Liberalism

Liberalism is a philosophy of government and is not concerned with private lives, apart from the responsibility of government and other public
institutions to provide the freedom, opportunities, and security needed for
the development of human potential. Beyond that, the liberal commitment to freedom leaves individuals responsible for their own lives. Exception is made for persons who cannot be held fully responsible, such as
children, the elderly, the disabled, etc. Liberals advocate courteous and
respectful treatment of everyone, without regard to age, race, or economic
circumstances. Freedom does not extend to persons whose actions threaten
or debase the lives and property of others.

Although Liberalism emphasizes the freedom and responsibility of the
individual, it has always assumed a social context. Aristotle described man
as "a social animal." John Locke posited a "state of nature" with "a law of
nature" that encouraged cooperation among individuals and included a
moral law. Locke's writings on toleration and education show his concern
for mutually satisfying and supportive social relationships. Adam Smith,
best known for his ideas on political economy, was a social philosopher
whose doctrine of "moral sentiments" explained morality and social rela-

tionships as based on the feelings of sympathy and mutual understanding developed by individuals living together in a community.

Near the end of his life, John Stuart Mill was concerned with the problem of poverty in a wealthy land. He concluded in his *Autobiography* that the problem of the future was to combine political and economic liberty (in his view largely achieved) with concern for the constraints that poverty imposes on individuals and families. In that respect he conceded that he had become something of a "socialist."

The Victorians were not indifferent to the vast social problems of their great industrial cities, but they did not expect their national government to do very much. They saw provision for the poor as a legal responsibility of the local community and a religious and moral obligation of individuals and churches. Dickens was a great humanitarian who depicted in vivid language the travails of the poor, but one will search in vain in his novels for appeals to government to intervene; he relied on individual character to rise above adversity, aided by charity and usually a lucky break.

William E. Gladstone, the great Liberal Prime Minister, advocated a small and economical central government. By the end of his long career, the Liberal Party had accepted increased intervention of the national government in some social issues. An important part of Disraeli's "Tory Democracy" was public efforts to improve housing and sanitation. Conservative efforts to improve education were hampered by quarrels between church-supported schools and the schools maintained by publicly supported school boards.

A great change in British Liberalism took place when the Liberal Party gained power in Britain in 1905. Faced with the growing problems of an industrialized and urbanized society, the Liberals accepted the view that individual freedom and dignity required the larger community to concern itself with meeting the minimum needs of all its members. The principle adopted was to provide both opportunity and security: "the ladder and the net."

"The New Liberalism" (1905–14) gave the central government a major role in dealing with social problems. One aspect of "the New Liberalism" was to secure for trade unions the right to strike. Without this leverage it was believed that the unions could not effectively carry out their role, which was to promote the well being of the industrial working class. Winston Churchill, at that time a Liberal, led in establishing boards to set wage guidelines for unorganized workers, thus introducing the equivalent of our minimum wage.

The Liberal government recognized that certain contingencies arose where low-income workers could not provide for themselves or their families. People grew old, and when they were old they could no longer work. People got sick and needed medical care. Workers were injured on the job and the family faced destitution. Unemployment was the nemesis of industrial workers. The Liberal "safety net" included old-age pensions, medical care, compensation for work-related injuries, and unemployment benefits.

These important steps toward the welfare state did not abrogate individual responsibility, a fundamental principle of the liberal creed. But British Liberals realized that the low wages of industrial Britain left little if anything to set aside for "a rainy day." The safety net would help out in those situations where individuals could not be held fully responsible. Apart from old age pensions, which were paid from the General Revenue, the Liberal Party did not abandon its commitment to low-cost, efficient government. Benefits were based on an insurance system paid for by contributions (like our Social Security taxes) from employers and workers.

After World War II, the British Labour Party established a partially socialist economy with a comprehensive welfare state. The earlier Liberal measures were extended to include everyone "from the cradle to the grave." It was found that some people abused the system, and turned the "safety net" into a hammock.

The induction of large numbers of young men and women into the military services during World War II had revealed the wretched state of health in Britain. For the first time in their lives, many of these young people received proper medical attention. When the war ended there was broad agreement that such a condition should never again exist.

The most dramatic accomplishment of the Labour government was the National Health Service, which provided free medical care (later small charges were introduced; for everyone. The National Health Service was an agency of the central government that provided complete health care, including doctors, dentists, and hospitals. Administratively, it was highly decentralized. Health Service doctors and hospitals were permitted to provide care to private patients on a fee-for-service basis.

At first the backlog of unmet needs was so great that the system was overwhelmed. Since that time the demands for medical care in the contemporary world have become so vast that some kind of rationing (usually waiting) has become necessary. Despite its deficiencies, the British people are strongly attached to the National Health Service, which is the commitment by their national government that they will never be without medical care, although they may have to wait for it.

Margaret Thatcher, Conservative Prime Minister from 1979–1990, was a free-market Liberal in her economic policies. Her main purpose was to open up "the ladder." She recognized the political realities and social needs of a modern industrialized state. She proposed broad reforms of the welfare state for purposes of efficiency and economy, but the principle of "the net" remained. Her policies were continued by John Major, her successor, and Tony Blair, leader of the Labour Party, who became Prime Minister in 1997.

The British welfare state raised questions that have plagued the American equivalent. One was financing: national insurance vs. funding from general revenue. The other was universality vs. programs based on need, which requires personal information ("means testing"). Universal provision is frightfully expensive, but politically it seems impossible to provide benefits to those who need them without giving them to millionaires too.

Social Liberalism in the United States

In the United States the development of Social Liberalism has followed the British model, but has been complicated by our deep-seated suspicion of central authority and the complexities of our federal system. As they developed a new nation, Americans learned to cooperate on a personal, family, or local level rather than looking to a distant central government in Washington. Social problems were dealt with by the county or township poor fund and by institutions such as churches, schools, colleges, hospitals, the YMCA and YWCA, settlement houses, and the Salvation Army. Many of those institutions continue to make important contributions today.

Americans were active joiners of reform movements to combat social evils such as drunkenness, prostitution, child labor, unsanitary foods, and medical quackery. These movements gave an outlet to the energies and dedication of middle-class women, who were always the leaders in the effort to civilize American life.

In the twentieth century, Americans began to realize that many of their social problems were national and required national solutions. With the rise of the United States as an industrial nation, American democracy was threatened by the social tensions that inevitably arise where great wealth and poverty exist side by side and where economic insecurity is rampant.

Liberals argued that freedom must mean more than Anatole France's wry definition: "the equal freedom of the rich and the poor to sleep under bridges." They decided that personal freedom and dignity in an industrial society required a decent standard of living for all. To achieve that goal, Liberals advocated a degree of federal involvement in social problems that contradicted the earlier liberal concern with minimal government and low taxes.

Although there were forerunners, Social Liberalism became established with the Great Depression. The shock of that disaster made it clear that the United States needed a safety net, and that the net could not be left to state and local governments. As part of Franklin Roosevelt's New Deal, the United States did essentially what the British Liberals had done before World War I. The Wagner Act guaranteed the rights of labor unions. The New Deal established the Social Security system, with old-age pensions, workmen's compensation, and unemployment benefits. As in Britain, the Social Security system was based on the principle of insurance, to which both employers and employees contributed.

The Depression resulted in other programs to deal with poverty and deprivation. Large public works provided jobs for the unemployed. The unseen rural poor were aided by programs to increase farm income. After World War II, the New Deal was extended by Harry Truman's Fair Deal and Lyndon Johnson's "Great Society" to include Medicare, Medicaid, and Aid to Families of Dependent Children. Johnson's "war on poverty" established a variety of programs to assist those who, for various reasons, were unable to support themselves at a decent level. Regrettably, his war in Vietnam gobbled up the political support and financial resources that he needed to get these programs off to a good start. Since then, Conservatives have used tax cuts for the wealthy and high military expenditures to weaken the liberal effort to reduce economic deprivation and social injustice.

These programs are the commitment of the American nation to support people who need help. Nothing could be more important to Liberals than to maintain this federal commitment. Under Pres. Bill Clinton, the Department of Health and Human Services began a process of administrative reform, delegating many responsibilities to the states but maintaining federal funding and guidelines. Many other worthwhile proposals for federal-state-local cooperation with federal funding have been made. The Liberal motto should be: "Mend it, don't end it."

Liberalism and Education

Liberalism accepts opportunity, as well as security, as a proper responsibility of government. The "safety net" cannot work without "the ladder." That means investments in education and social services that will help our people lead productive and satisfying lives.

The public schools are one of the great achievements of American liberal democracy. Even before our federal government was formed, a system of public schools was seen as essential to a self-governing nation. The Land Ordinance of 1785, drafted by Thomas Jefferson, devoted one section in every township to public schools. The Lincoln administration established the land-grant universities.

The commitment of Americans to a federal investment in education was most notably displayed in the GI Bill of Rights, which supported the education of several million veterans [including the author of this book]. It was the best investment made by our federal government since the Louisiana Purchase. Since then, federal programs have given support to schools in a variety of ways. The liberal principle of federal aid to education is now well established.

Nevertheless, the public schools have been primarily the concern of state and local governments. Without denigrating the role of private schools, the public schools are still the principal agents in our educational system, and as such they are the bedrock of our society. They disseminate a body of knowledge and skills that unite us as Americans. They have been one of the core institutions in Americanizing the immigrants from many cultures who continue to flow into this country.

The strongest objections to the federal role in education come from Conservatives, who refuse to recognize the importance of the public school as a democratizing, unifying, and civilizing force in American life. They will, if they get their way, destroy one of the fundamental institutions that made America different, and arguably better. That's conservative? Defending and improving the public schools must remain high on the liberal agenda.

One of the great changes of our time has been the enormous increase in higher education. At present, a majority of high school graduates expect to attend a university, college, junior (community) college, or some institution offering career-oriented advanced training. This aspiration fits perfectly into the liberal commitment to personal opportunity and national strength and unity. America in the twenty-first century requires advanced education for careers, personal development, and good citizenship. The cost of higher education is great, and needs to be spread among the federal government, the states, and individuals and their families. The liberal sense of fairness requires that educational opportunities should be available to disadvantaged students without regard to gender, race, creed, or national origin.

Liberalism and Poverty

Liberal institutions exist to enable individuals to lead productive and satisfying lives. Liberals advocate public efforts to provide opportunities and remove obstacles to personal fulfillment. Liberal anti-poverty programs are intended to give hope and encouragement, and this should continue to be the liberal goal. Few people actually spend a lifetime on welfare, but at times they may require assistance and encouragement to get back on their feet again.

The Clinton administration's principle of welfare reform was to encourage people to work by "making work pay." The most effective of the anti-poverty programs is the Earned Income Tax Credit, which encourages work by supplementing the income of people who work full time and still fall below the poverty line. Nothing is more important than to encourage the work ethic among low-income people who otherwise would end up on welfare.

Many of America's social problems grow out of the large number of single mothers. The largest proportion of people living at or below the poverty line are single mothers struggling to make ends meet while raising children. The most important objective must be to enable single mothers to work. They cannot leave welfare if it means losing their child benefits and Medicaid card. Childcare must be provided to make it possible for single mothers to hold jobs or pursue training that will lead to employment.

The federal role should be to establish standards of support for single parents and their children, and provide funding to help state and local governments meet them. Considering the mobility of our people and jobs, it should be apparent to all but conservative ideologues that we can no longer afford wide state and regional variations in the opportunities we provide for the children of poverty.

Liberalism and Race

Some of the most difficult social problems in our country arise out of race, and the problems of race are rooted in slavery. Thomas Jefferson, although himself a slave-holder, recognized the violation of human rights on which slavery was based, but he felt powerless to do anything about it. Abraham Lincoln, who had no doubt that slavery was an evil, was reluctant to raise the issue when the Civil War began. Some opponents of slavery thought it best to let the South secede, thus removing the monstrosity from our republic. Lincoln decided to preserve the Union, and when he did so he sounded the death knell of slavery, for he himself had defined the issue: the union could not continue half-slave and half free.

Slavery was replaced by segregation: economic and social segregation in the North, plus legal segregation in the South. Living within those limitations, African-Americans developed a culture of their own. They had their own doctors, lawyers, ministers, teachers, churches and colleges. Life was poor and hard for most African-Americans, but they had their own family and social networks that cared for the children, the elderly, and people who needed help.

Franklin Roosevelt and the New Deal brought federal programs to African-Americans, including jobs on federal work projects, relief payments, and Social Security. World War II brought African-Americans into the armed services and led large numbers of African-Americans to the cities of the North and the West Coast to work in defense plants. After the war, the invention of the cotton-picking machine and herbicides eliminated hoeing and picking cotton—the basis of African-American life in the Deep South. Northward they came, a huge migration from a part of the country that was, in some respects, part of the Third World.

Liberalism, with its respect for human dignity and freedom, is philosophically opposed to racial discrimination. American Liberals, including African-American Liberals like Martin Luther King, were the principal agents in bringing an end to institutionalized racism. The Civil Rights Act (1964) opened hotels, restaurants, and other public facilities to everyone, regardless of race. The Voting Rights Act (1965) guaranteed the vote to black voters, where it had been denied by state or local regulations.

Liberals were also active in attempting to overcome informal discrimination. The civil rights movement brought equal political and legal rights to African-Americans, but the racial attitudes and mores of mainstream America were not readily changed. To break down these attitudes, agitation and education were necessary, supported by anti-discrimination laws and the talents and determination of African-Americans themselves.

Liberals should agree that this process has met with considerable success. Since the 1960s the number of African-Americans in the middle class has greatly increased: they hold steady jobs in business, government, education, the military, police forces, and hospitals; they participate in professional organizations; they hold elective offices and are prominent in sports and music.

In polite society, racist attitudes and conduct are taboo, or at least regarded as in bad taste African-Americans circulate freely with whites, not only in public places but in employment, mixed neighborhoods, and professional organizations. Although sharp regional variations exist, whites and blacks normally get along well enough for all practical purposes. Celebrities like Colin Powell, Bill Cosby, Michael Jordan, and Tiger Woods are not identified racially (nor do they make a point of it) but are accepted as American high achievers.

Liberalism and Immigration

The United States is a nation descended from immigrants, and immigration continues high, although the origins of the immigrants have changed dramatically over the years. The foundation of the American population is northern European, principally British, Irish, German, and Scandinavian. In the early twentieth century large immigrations came from the Mediterranean countries and Eastern Europe. Before and after World War II, European refugees (many of them Jews) provided large numbers of well-educated people who contributed immeasurably to the intellectual, scientific, and cultural life of this country. Since then, Asia and Latin America have provided the majority of immigrants, most of whom have found places in American life.

Today immigration creates a dilemma for Liberals. Liberal idealism and humanitarianism encourage them to welcome immigrants. The contribution of immigrants to the economy is important. American civilization has been enormously enriched by the wide variety of immigrants who have settled here, bringing with them the cultures of their native lands. But Liberal Realism suggests that there is a limit to the number of immigrants that America can absorb without endangering the civilization that undergirds this nation.

Regrettably, extensive immigration has also contributed to a politics of ethnicity far removed from the liberal sense of responsible citizenship and national unity. Ambitious politicians cultivate ethnic groups to provide an electoral base to promote their own ambitions. To some extent, this has always been true in America, and it is seen by some as a step toward assimilation. Nevertheless, if the United States is to remain a democracy, its immigrants must think and vote as Americans, not as members of an ethnic group.

Education is especially important in respect to immigration. Americans assume that immigrants intend to become citizens of the United States, and participate fully in the benefits and obligations of citizenship. Education, including adult education, plays an essential role in this process, and this is another reason for a strong system of public schools and universities. Our powerful popular culture contributes to Americanization, but sometimes in ways that may not be conducive to good citizenship.

The main questions about immigration are complicated by illegal immigration. It is very important that every country control its own borders, not only in respect to immigrants but also to deal with terrorism, crime and drugs. It is time for Liberals to consider where they stand on immigration. There will have to be a trade-off between Liberal Idealism and the realities of a harsh world, where millions of desperate people seek access to the United States. In short—Liberal Realism. Liberal Nationalism dictates that the decision be based upon the needs of the United States, not some imagined global responsibility for the fate of mankind. Or that part of mankind that gets its problems on TV.

Liberalism and Women

As advocates of personal freedom and opportunity, Liberals have actively promoted the striking changes in the roles of women that have taken place in the past half-century. The middle class has experienced an almost total reversal of the traditional expectation that women marry and stay at home to care for the family. Most middle-class young women expect to be educated and have a career, with or without a husband and children. In general, the new role for women has been a positive force in our national life. Our progressive, affluent country would be impossible without the active involvement of women.

The modern feminist movement began in the mid-nineteenth century with demands for political and legal equality for women, including the vote, which was granted by the Nineteenth Amendment in 1920. The movement for full legal equality was embodied in the unsuccessful Equal Rights Amendment, but those goals have largely been achieved in other ways. Conservatives cleverly turned the campaign for the Equal Rights Amendment away from democratic rights (where the feminists held the winning hand) into a debate over changing gender roles. This approach had considerable appeal to women of the older generation, some of whom felt that their lives as homemakers were denigrated by career women, or perhaps they regretted that they had missed out.

Present-day feminist organizations are overwhelmingly middle class, and they have concentrated on middle-class complaints. However, the major problems of women these days are those of poor women, especially single-parent families headed by women. Although two responsible and caring parents are usually preferable to one, it has now become necessary to accept the single-parent family where it exists and make the best of it. Feminists should concern themselves less with the glass ceiling and more with the dirt floor.

The needs of single mothers bring us back again to anti-poverty programs and the safety net. Conservatives speak much and eloquently about the importance of the family and "family values," but they become strangely silent when confronted with the needs of the low-income single-parent family. As always, the responsibility rests with Liberals.

Liberalism and the Elderly

Among the first steps taken by Liberals, in Britain and America, to meet the needs of those who could not be expected to provide for themselves, were old-age pensions. Since then, the major beneficiaries of the American safety net have been the elderly. Their children benefit indirectly in that they are relieved of some of the burden of providing for their parents. Employer pension-plans, Social Security, Medicare, and Medicaid have largely eliminated destitution among senior citizens, and have enabled many to maintain their homes and lifestyles.

Outlays for Social Security pensions will increase greatly in the next few years with the retirement of the Baby Boomers and increasing longevity. The costs of Medicare and Medicaid continue to grow rapidly, and will increase even more with the addition of a Prescription Drug Benefit. It is apparent that something needs to be done to control the costs of health care for the elderly. It should be Liberals—who established these programs and truly believe in their value—who should come forward with sound proposals.

In addition to the problem of future funding, it is essential to realize the great distortions that the present Social Security system introduces into the American economy. Social Security taxes are a tax on jobs, paid by employers and employees. Furthermore, payroll taxes are our most regressive taxes, falling disproportionately on lower-income workers and families. Additionally, most employers provide medical insurance for their employees. In a globalized market, our businesses have to bear a burden that competitors in many other countries do not. It is difficult to create more jobs if employers have to absorb high payroll taxes and provide medical insurance. This burden should not be placed on the productive part of our economy. A different form of funding for these essential programs must be found.

Liberalism and Crime

Crime has been with the human race ever since Cain and Abel, and all societies find it necessary to develop institutions to prevent crime and punish criminals. Crime has been worse in the United States than in many advanced countries due to our individualism and materialism, the complexity of our system of law enforcement and corrections, and the pervasive presence of firearms. Nevertheless, most Americans are reasonably satisfied with our criminal justice system, despite its high cost, tedious procedures, instances of unfairness, and occasional brutality.

Liberals believe in the rule of law, and Liberals have been the leaders in insisting on fair trials and decent treatment of persons accused of crime. Conservatives have accused Liberals of "coddling criminals," but fair criminal procedures are important to everyone. Our criminal procedures are still badly flawed and require continuing examination and reform in the interests of justice, including justice for defendants.

Conservatives claim to be "tough on crime," but they refuse to vote the taxes needed to maintain strong law enforcement and deal with the causes of crime. Their view is "lock 'em up and throw away the key." They favor the death penalty, which accomplishes nothing, and they make life more hazardous for the police by opposing control of handguns and automatic weapons.

Organized crime is a special case. Organized crime was fostered by the restrictions on alcohol during Prohibition (1919–33), and now is supported primarily by the distribution of addictive drugs. Although both drugs and alcohol are social scourges, attempts to control their use by prohibition have failed. Like Prohibition, drug laws have corrupted law enforcement officials and have created new kinds of criminals: those who provide the drugs, and the addicts who commit crimes to pay for them. Our present drug laws are based on cutting off the supply. They have not worked, and when they do work the only effect is to drive up prices. As long as the demand is there, the supply will be provided. A new approach is needed.

Liberals should also turn their attention to our dysfunctional prison system. The American reliance on imprisonment as punishment, and perhaps as a place of rehabilitation, is enormously costly. Prisons complicate the problem of crime, since they have become schools for criminals and the incidence of recidivism is high. Some prison programs that deal with non-violent criminals have had modest success, and these should be continued and improved. For individuals whose chances of leading a law-abiding life are good, parole with electronic surveillance can be an effective alternative to prison.

Is American Society Failing?

Everyone knows that American society is changing rapidly. But is it changing for the better? Or for worse? Does our democracy function effectively for all our people while checking abuses of political or economic power? Are our people better informed and more responsible as citizens? Is our national unity stronger and more firmly based? Are our people being pre-pared to function effectively in a competitive, market-based global econ-omy? Does our society hold together on essentials while accepting our diversities? Do we care adequately for the most dependent and helpless among us? Do we cherish American civilization while seeking ways to strengthen and improve it?

These are the questions that Liberals should ask. Social Liberalism con-sists of positive approaches to these questions. In this present age of nega-tivism, it is important that the liberal answer to the above questions will always be "we're working on it!"

9

Bill Clinton: The Way Forward or Dead End?

Bill Clinton and his counterpart in Britain, Tony Blair, who had studied the Clinton presidency closely, were on the right track. They were developing a consensus Liberalism suitable for a prosperous, advanced society with a broad middle class and a working class with middle-class values and aspirations. They had grasped the essential principles of Liberalism, and they made an effort to avoid the contentious, special-interest issues that had become attached to the liberal message.

The Man and the Candidate

Bill Clinton was superbly qualified by his talents to be president of the United States. He was exceptionally intelligent, with a remarkable ability to master a wide range of ideas and information. He was tall, handsome, and superbly articulate especially when speaking off the cuff. He had a wonderful ability to relate to people in small groups or large. He had received an excellent education at Georgetown, Yale Law School, and Oxford. From his youth intended to be president, and he made it.

But talent is not everything. Clinton's experience of life and politics prior to his presidency was sadly deficient. He grew up in Hot Springs, Arkansas, a decayed spa replete with gambling, prostitution, and other vices. His disturbed family did not give him the ethical values that are fostered in a good home. As he came of age, his charm gave him easy access to women, his one vice. It should be said that he never showed other vices, such as avarice, alcoholism or gambling. He probably regarded sex as a game that he was good at, an attitude not unusual among the youth of the 1960s.

Bill Clinton should be understood as a character common in fiction—the ambitious young man of low social origins who uses his talents and energy to rise to the top. If not born in a log cabin, the hillbilly state of Arkansas can be regarded as a modern equivalent. He saw that he could succeed in politics, and he based his politics on pleasing people and winning their confidence—a talent that he possessed in abundance. He looked great in a tuxedo and delighted in associating with elites of wealth, talent, and celebrity, who regarded him as one of them. His rise and fall were a tale fit for a novel by F. Scott Fitzgerald.

Clinton's desire to please was not just a political tactic. It was part of his personality. In a TV interview, he was asked about the incident when he, as a teenager, confronted his alcoholic stepfather to protect his mother from abuse. When the interviewer asked how this episode might have influenced him, he replied that, as much as possible, he sought to avoid conflict and confrontations and to resolve differences peaceably.

Clinton could be courageous when necessary, as when he presented a budget message in 1993 that raised taxes. He delayed his promised middle-class tax cut to increase the Earned Income Tax Credit, a benefit to low-income people that few understood or appreciated. But much of the time he aggravated his friends and encouraged his enemies by his reluctance to be pinned down if an immediate decision could be avoided.

Clinton held the typical Liberal ideals of the 1960s, with a genuine concern for poor people. He exhibited remarkable rapport with African-Americans. His political instincts and Liberal ideals led to his association with "the New Democrats" of the Democratic Leadership Council. Politically, the New Democrats avoided the old formulas (rich vs. poor—capital vs. labor) that had shaped the Democratic Party in the days of FDR and Truman. They knew that elections were won by appealing to the broad middle class that had become the dominant force in American life in the half-century since World War II.

However, in the 1960s many Liberals had advocated radical social causes that had driven moderate Democrats (Reagan Democrats) into the

Republican Party. Opposition to the Vietnam War had given the Democrats the reputation of peaceniks who were unwilling to use force to defend national interests abroad. Federal civil rights legislation had turned many Southerners into Republicans. The radical Right, which was especially strong in the South and West, kept up an unceasing attack on the mythical demons that they referred to loosely as "librals."

The New Democrats sought to win back the moderates by adopting policies that would restore consensus Liberalism, while turning their backs on the contentious clamors of the "New Left," including the strident black leaders who had captured and distorted the civil rights movement. The reasonableness and moderation of the New Democrats were appealing to Clinton, whose instinctive desire to resolve differences by moderation and compromise was strengthened by his recognition of the political viability of the movement.

Clinton's wife, Hillary, was an asset in that she was intelligent, well educated, and as absorbed in politics as he was. She supported him, financially and otherwise, in the pursuit of their mutual ambition to reach the White House. At times she may have compensated for the lack of political courage that her husband often displayed, and she put up with a lot as his wife. She was unquestionably helpful in dealing with Democratic officials and organizations when the Clintons extended their ambitions beyond Arkansas. As a lawyer in Little Rock, Hillary was involved with some sleazy people, but there is no reason to think the she was other than honest and straightforward. The famous Whitewater case, beaten to death by the Republicans, was little more than a failed land deal, in which the Clintons, naive in such matters, had been badly advised.

The main problem was that the Clintons had no money, a crucial factor in the shaping of their approach to politics. Clinton's incessant hunger for money was the result of the corruption of American elections, especially at the national level. Talents, dedication, energy, and ambition, he knew, were nothing without money—lots of it! Many of the unseemly aspects of Bill Clinton's career grew out of this political imperative.

The Clintons were carpetbaggers when they entered the presidential sweepstakes. They needed free TV coverage until the time that their candidacy gained enough momentum to garner campaign contributions. It was touch and go at first, but Clinton's charm captured the attention of the networks, which look for freshness and novelty and were tired of covering the usual suspects. The Gennifer Flowers sex scandal got Clinton on *"Sixty Minutes,"* with Hilary by his side. When people began to take notice, his talents and energy became evident.

He benefited from the reluctance of Democratic heavyweights to enter the primaries. After the Gulf War in 1991, the ratings of Pres. George Herbert Bush soared into the stratosphere, and he seemed unbeatable. Bush's ratings fell as another world recession set in, but by then it was too late for prestigious Democrats to enter the field. The Clintons, who had nothing to lose, were already in the race, and challenges from other candidates were swept aside.

Clinton was also assisted by the independent candidacy of Ross Perot, whose frankness and attention to substantive issues—the budget and the debt—reminded people of Harry Truman. Perot's campaign forced the other candidates to respond to these issues, but the public realized that he was there first and was indubitably sincere. Perot received 21 percent of the vote in the election, and his race enabled Clinton to win with 43 percent.

Clinton never got over the incessant need for TV attention, which was partially personal egotism and partially a political tactic. As president, his political advisers developed the concept of "the continuous campaign," with a constant flow of pronouncements and photo-ops. The spin-doctor, always putting a White House slant on the news, was the face and voice of the administration. The Clintons loved to hobnob with celebrities, who brought with them a different kind of limelight. The dignity and mystery of the presidency were sacrificed to media exposure.

The President

When Bill Clinton reached the White House, he learned the hard way that his political experience in Arkansas and the doctrines of the New Democrats were inadequate to meet the challenges he faced as a national leader. Arkansas politics were narrow and corrupt, and he had not developed the political skills that might be expected from the governor of a large state, who would have been called upon to deal with a variety of issues and interest groups. The broad highway of the New Democrats, he discovered, was littered with the potholes, roadblocks, and detours generated by party politics, interest groups, and the U. S. constitution.

The first two years of the Clinton presidency were marked by political floundering, mixed messages, and an indiscriminate advocacy of favorite Liberal causes. The main accomplishment was a counter-inflationary budget that included a tax increase, always an unpopular measure, as Pres. Bush had discovered two years earlier. The budget passed the Senate by the casting vote of Vice President Al Gore. The Bush and Clinton tax increases, jointly, restored the irresponsible tax cuts of Reaganism and put the federal government on the way to solvency.

The Clinton administration adopted economic policies that encouraged economic growth. International economic institutions, such as the International Monetary Fund and World Bank were strengthened. The General Agreement on Tariffs and Trade (GATT) opened markets and established the World Trade Organization to resolve differences. Clinton signed the treaty establishing NAFTA (the North American Free Trade Association) to open up trade between the United States, Canada, and Mexico. The United States contributed substantially to bailouts of the Mexican and Southeast Asian economies, which were followed by reforms monitored by the International Monetary Fund.

The first term was marked by a political disaster, the Federal Health Insurance Program presented to Congress by First Lady Hilary Clinton, who reveled in the opportunity to play a part in the political game. Nothing was more revealing of the amateurism of the Clinton administration than the lack of political realism in the content of the bill and the absence of broadly based consultation and effective presentation.

The Health Care Bill would provide comprehensive health care to people not covered already. Federal purchasing cooperatives would be established to contract with hospitals and pharmaceutical companies to provide their services at reasonable prices. The administration claimed that the savings made by the purchasing cooperatives would cover the cost of the uninsured, while people with health insurance would be no worse off than before.

Although the legislation had some merits in theory, opposition was so intense and diverse that it did not stand a chance in Congress. Approximately 80 percent of Americans were insured and were satisfied with the health insurance that they had. They were reluctant to risk their coverage to help the millions of people who were uninsured. After the debacle, small but valuable steps were taken by the Kennedy-Kassebaum Act (1996), which provided for portability of health insurance from one employer to another. A federal program was established (1998) to provide health care for poor children. A Patient's Bill of Rights (1998) may have been of some value.

It retrospect, it is evident that the centerpiece of Clinton's first two years should have been welfare reform. He had promised to "end welfare as we know it." Well-considered legislation on this matter would have received widespread public support, since most people were not on welfare and many resented the people who were. The bill would have been considered by a Congress where the Democrats controlled both houses, and the interests of the poor and indigent would have received careful consideration. When welfare reform was considered two years later, political conditions had changed dramatically.

Clinton's floundering in his first two years brought a backlash in the off-year election of 1994, when Newt Gingrich and the radical Republicans, united behind a document called *The Contract with America*, which few people had ever seen, gained control of Congress for the first time in forty years. Regrettably, welfare reform fell to Gingrich and his radical Republicans and was approved by Clinton as he prepared to run for a second term. The key feature of the bill was to abolish Aid to Families with Dependent Children and cast the burden on the states, with a federally funded five-year transition period. After that, the states and the children were on their own. In short, single mothers paid the price for Clinton's re-election.

Fortunately for Clinton, the Gingrich Republicans discredited themselves as extremists, both rhetorically and legislatively, especially when they used their control of the budgetary process to shut down the federal government. Gingrich compounded his problems by his own triumphalism and personal excesses. When Clinton vetoed the Gingrich budget, public opinion began to rally to his support, and Clinton had learned something about the political value of courage.

Clinton's victory over a weak Republican candidate in 1996 gave him the political and public mandate that he had lacked in his first term. The main achievement was the Balanced Budget Act (1997), which included budget caps and a variety of tax reforms and spending cuts. The new Liberal Economics worked. With peace abroad, federal deficits replaced by a surplus, and a stable dollar, interest rates fell. Employer and consumer confidence bounced back. Investment (foreign and domestic) soared, and investment sparked economic growth. A bubble arose in the stock market, but growth in the real economy was substantial. Clinton's Earned Income Tax Credit and welfare reform reduced the incentives to welfare dependence, and the buoyant economy provided millions of new jobs. Health-care and childcare for single mothers enabled them to leave the welfare rolls for paid employment.

World Leader

Clinton was committed to restraint in foreign policy, which was essential to his fiscal and economic policies. Like most governors who become president, he had no experience in foreign policy. He took many trips abroad to gain acceptance as a world statesman. He attempted to work with Boris Yeltsin, the erratic president of Russia, to bring some stability to that country, still reeling from the shock of the breakdown of the Soviet Union. He encouraged expansion of NATO to Eastern Europe, and supported the efforts of the British government to bring peace to Northern Ireland. Warren Christopher, Secretary of State, spent much of his time in the first term attempting to resolve the Israeli-Palestinian conflict.

Clinton enforced the decision of the Gulf War by conducting (with the British) flights over the Kurdish and Shi'ite no-fly zones of Iraq. When Saddam Hussein stealthily began rebuilding his military forces, Clinton joined with Tony Blair, the new British prime minister, in a bombing campaign intended to destroy Saddam's facilities to develop chemical and biological weapons.

One trouble spot in Eastern Europe was Yugoslavia, which in 1991 broke into its constituent parts. War broke out between Croatia, supported by Germany and most of the West, and Serbia, which had inherited the capital (Belgrade) and army of Yugoslavia. Brutal ethnic conflict took place between Croats and Serbs, in which the major culprit was Slobodan Milosovic, leader of Serbia, although his Croatian counterpart engaged in similar tactics. The U. N. Security Council imposed economic sanctions on Serbia, which, of course, did not end the conflict but made life more difficult for ordinary people. After savage fighting and "ethnic cleansing," a peace was signed in 1995 that gave most of the disputed territories to Croatia. Millions of refugees sought new homes in Eastern and Western Europe or other parts of the Balkans.

The Balkan crisis came to a head in Bosnia, which was populated by Croats, Serbs, and a Moslem minority centered in the city of Sarajevo, a popular tourist resort and site of the 1984 Winter Olympic Games. When Bosnia declared its independence from Serbia in 1991, Serb militiamen, provided with ample ammunition by Milosovic, began shelling Sarajevo from the surrounding mountains. Savage fighting broke out among the three ethnic groups. A United Nations military force, comprised mainly of British and French troops, was sent to Bosnia as peacekeepers, but since there was no peace, they were ineffective. The U. S. Army, still bound to the Powell doctrine, was reluctant to become involved in a Balkan civil war.

Televised scenes of ethnic cleansing were intolerable to the governments and peoples of the West. Furthermore, Western Europe faced another flood of Eastern European refugees. In 1995 Clinton, responding to the pleas of the European allies, authorized massive NATO air strikes, primarily American, against the Serb militiamen in Bosnia, who took to their heels at the first sign of danger. This intervention brought the fighting to a halt and a peace conference, brokered by the United States, was held in Dayton OH. The Dayton agreement papered-over bitter ethnic conflicts and established an independent, multi-ethnic Bosnia where people who hated each other were expected to live together peaceably. NATO stationed 60,000 troops (20,000 of them American) in Bosnia and the fighting stopped. Bosnia languished within its unworkable constitutional framework, and the media turned to other crises. In 1999 a massive corruption scandal revealed that much of the $5.1 in aid sent for reconstruction and humanitarian purposes had been embezzled.

At this point Milosovic turned his attention to Kosovo, a part of former Yugoslavia claimed by the Serbs for historical reasons but with an Albanian (Moslem) majority. In 1997, attacks by the Kosovo Liberation Army, a rag-tag force comprised of Albanians, led Milosovic to undertake a counter-offensive by the Serbian army, including violent "ethnic cleansing." Hundreds of thousands of Kosovar Albanians fled to seek refuge in neighboring countries. Clinton was reluctant to intervene in civil and ethnic conflicts, which did not lend themselves to military solutions and were likely to produce a political backlash. U. S. military leaders shared this view and opposed the introduction of ground forces into such an intractable situation, but were willing to attack from the air.

Britain's Tony Blair insisted that there was a moral obligation to stop ethnic cleansing, an appeal that carried considerable weight with Clinton. In response to Blair and world opinion, Clinton unleashed an intense bombing campaign against Belgrade, capital of Serbia (Yugoslavia), and other Serbian targets, which did great damage to innocent civilians without getting rid of the dictator. The destruction of the Danube bridges was a disaster to the commerce of the entire Danube Basin, not just Serbia. A "smart" missile hit the Chinese embassy. The missile was smart but the targeters were not; they had identified the wrong building. The Albanians returned to Kosovo and began an ethnic cleansing of the Serbs. At that point, NATO sent 50,000 troops, including Americans, to establish an uneasy peace. Eventually Milosovic was ousted by his own people in a scheduled election, and is now on trial as a war criminal. Despite the presence of NATO peacekeepers, Albanian attacks on the remaining Serbs continued, and Kosovo is now overwhelmingly Albanian.

The interventions of NATO in the Balkan conflicts provided a new role for NATO as a force to preserve order in Europe. Since NATO relied primarily on American airpower and needed American troops for peacekeeping duties, Clinton's Balkan interventions may be justified as a proper use of American military power in that they strengthened the relationship of America with its European Allies. Whether these interventions actually improved the lives of the Balkan peoples is questionable. Tony Blair, British Prime Minister, who had been the major figure in persuading Clinton to undertake the Kosovo intervention, saw it as a triumph for human rights, in that it stopped Serbian ethnic cleansing and contributed to the overthrow of a brutal dictator.

Clinton became increasingly concerned about the threat of international terrorism, especially the operations of Osama Bin Laden and other Arab terrorists associated with him. In 1993, Arab terrorists set off a bomb in the World Trade Center that caused great damage, although the towers did not collapse and were promptly repaired. In 1996 terrorists attacked an American barracks in Saudi Arabia, killing 19. In 1996 they bombed American embassies in Kenya and Tanzania, killing 263 people, mainly Africans. In 2000 they attacked the *USS Cole* in the Red Sea, killing 17 American sailors.

In Clinton's second term, terrorism became the No. 1 national security interest of the administration. Recognizing the difficulties of using military force in Afghanistan, Clinton was unwilling to risk American lives in risky attempts to capture or kill Osama Bin Laden. American military leaders were equally reluctant; they were set up to wage wars, they said, not get involved in counter-terrorism activities. The FBI saw terrorism as a domestic, law-enforcement concern, and the CIA collected intelligence but was chary about covert operations against such an elusive target.

Clinton fought back at long range. On several occasions cruise missiles were fired at meetings called by Bin Laden, but he escaped unscathed. In 1996 cruise missiles were fired at one of Bin Laden's camps in Afghanistan, but the camp could easily be replaced. Innocent lives were lost when a pharmaceutical plant in the Sudan that was mistakenly suspected of manufacturing materials for bio-terrorism was attacked with cruise missiles. These unsuccessful attacks only enhanced the reputation of Osama Bin Laden in the Arab world. When the Bush administration took office in January 2001, intelligence experts insisted on the urgency of a coordinated international effort to destroy Bin Laden and defend against terrorism. At that time, Bush was more interested in war against the regime of Saddam Hussein in Iraq, which was not involved in terrorist activities.

Clinton's presidency ended on a sour note, as an independent prosecutor appointed by Congress revealed details of his sexual dalliances with a young White House intern. He was also sued by a former employee of the State of Arkansas for an unwanted sexual advance. Clinton's ambiguous testimony in court, as he sought to avoid admitting his shabby conduct, verged on perjury and led to an attempt at impeachment that failed in the Senate. After the Lewinsky scandal and the impeachment, Clinton's poll numbers remained surprisingly high, but he had become a figure of ridicule. He had worn out his welcome.

Assessment

Bill Clinton and his counterpart in Britain, Tony Blair, who had studied the Clinton presidency closely, were on the right track. They were developing a consensus Liberalism suitable for a prosperous, advanced society with a broad middle class and a working class with middle-class values and aspirations. They had grasped the essential principles of Liberalism, and they made an effort to avoid the contentious, special-interest issues that had become attached to the liberal message. Blair's task was more difficult, because he had to transform a class-based, socialist Labour Party, which had never been the case with the Democratic Party.

Clinton was a better president than many people gave him credit for, but his personal shortcomings kept him from being the great president that his talents suggested. He developed and implemented a centrist, modern vision of Liberalism that had the potential to give the Democratic Party a broad-based appeal that it had lost in the 1970s. Clinton was uncomfortable using military force, but his military involvements in the Balkans and Kosovo weakened the image of the Democrats as peaceniks who were unwilling to use force when necessary.

Clinton's greatest failure was in passing on the baton to his successor. The defeat of Al Gore in the disputed election of 2000 was largely due to

Gore's ineptness as a campaigner, although confusion and fraud in the Florida election tipped the balance. That, in itself, did not determine the outcome. A broad swathe of respectable, middle-class Americans was determined to punish Bill Clinton for his sins. Although Gore had always been a straight arrow type, he became the scapegoat and their wrath fell on him. Gore, who was fully aware of the public attitude toward Clinton, was determined to avoid all identification with the disgraced president. He refused to campaign on his most important qualification—the obvious successes of the Clinton administration and his experience as part of that administration.

The effect of Gore's defeat was to stop in its tracks the revival and re-definition of Liberalism that Bill Clinton had begun. The Liberalism of Roosevelt, Truman, Kennedy, and Johnson had run its course. Given the flourishing condition of the country, there was good reason to believe that a new form of Liberalism was emerging that would restore Liberalism to the dominant role that it had exercised in most of the twentieth century. Instead, the Clinton presidency left few permanent marks. Peace abroad and prosperity at home were Clinton's most notable, and apparently tran-sient, accomplishments.

10

George W. Bush and the New Conservatism

The new Conservatism is "big-government Conservatism." Bush heads an activist administration with two main concerns: exerting American power throughout the world, and strengthening the political and financial power of individual and corporate wealth.

"Big-government Conservatism"

The presidency of George W. Bush is not "Conservative" in the conventional sense of political leadership that seeks stability and opposes innovation. Nor is the Bush administration Republican, traditionally understood as a party that advocates limited government, fiscal responsibility, efficient administration, and caution abroad. Ronald Reagan spoke the Republican rhetoric of rolling back the size, cost, and intrusiveness of the federal government, but he got nowhere, because he wanted to intensify the armaments race and the American people wanted a large federal government that did things for THEM. Bush and the new Conservatives have finally abandoned the small government rhetoric that for decades had activated the Republican base, no matter how much violated in practice.

The new Conservatism is "big-government Conservatism." Bush heads an activist administration with two main concerns: exerting American power throughout the world, and strengthening the political and financial power of individual and corporate wealth. The ideas behind the new Conservatism have been forged in well-financed, ideologically committed think tanks, located primarily in the Washington area, and charged with developing "bold new ideas" for the Conservative agenda. They have pushed actively to increase the role of private providers in Medicare and Social Security. Their most important "bold new idea" was the Messianic notion that the United States possesses the power, wisdom, and resources to bring "regime change" to crumbling "rogue states," whose culture we do not understand and whose people will resent our presence.

The fiscal policy of the new Conservatism is based on the obsolete belief that tax cuts and deficits will stimulate economic growth and eventually balance the budget. As the Clinton boom reached its peak, the stock market bubble burst and the real economy underwent a modest contraction. These are the normal corrective measures of healthy capitalism, and should have been taken in stride with a few tweaks here and there. Nevertheless, the Bush administration adopted a policy of "supply side economics," which included massive tax cuts for corporations and wealthy individuals and large increases in defense expenditures. The predictable result was unprecedented federal deficits.

Although these measures may have some immediate effect, a recovery based on public and consumer debt cannot last. As the stock market sagged and the economy languished in a slow recovery, Vice President Richard Cheney stated confidently: "Ronald Reagan demonstrated that deficits don't matter." As the elder Pres. Bush discovered to his dismay, they did.

The administration has been shameless in advocating legislation tailored to the needs of favored constituencies. Their plans for reform of Social Security include bringing insurance companies and other private interests into these programs. The failed Energy Bill included large subsidies and concessions to energy companies and other special interests. Environmental restrictions have been rolled back in favor of polluters of the air and water and exploiters of the public lands. Federal aid to education has wide popular appeal, but the administration's No Child Left Behind Act cannot be implemented without massive federal support, which is effectively foreclosed by Bush's tax cuts and expenditures for war and defense. Election politics is the only explanation for proposals to put a man on Mars and pass a constitutional amendment against gay marriages.

Well aware of electoral imperatives, the Bush administration expanded the welfare state by supporting legislation that added a prescription drug benefit to Medicare, while gratifying powerful contributors by including huge benefits to HMOs and pharmaceutical companies. The *Wall Street Journal* was appalled, and called the bill "too expensive a gamble for principled conservatives to support."

This shift to big government in domestic programs has not gone unchallenged within Conservative ranks, including such Conservative stalwarts as George Will, Rush Limbaugh, Dick Armey, and Conservative think tanks such as the Heritage Foundation and the Cato Institute. These Conservatives have criticized huge budget deficits and expanded federal commitments to Medicare and education as abandonment of Conservative principles. There have been murmurings of discontent among Republicans in Congress. It is likely that many sensible, moderate Republicans do not fully understand the radical change that has taken place in the national leadership of the party to which they maintain a long-standing loyalty.

Global Hegemony

The centerpiece of the new Conservatism is a vision of the United States as the supreme military power exercising an active foreign policy throughout the world, backed up by overwhelming military force. This sense of omnipotence is not only based on false premises; it is also likely to exact a heavy price.

Fate provided a rationalization for this new role on Sept. 11, 2001, when Arab terrorists from Afghanistan flew two airliners into the World Trade Center in New York, resulting in a spectacular collapse and fire. Another airliner hit the Pentagon and inflicted modest damage, while a fourth fell short of its goal and crashed. Bush, whose leadership until that time had been lackadaisical, suddenly found a role that he relished—"war president." He declared that the United States was at war, and most of the nation, stunned by the disaster, agreed. Elaborate provisions for domestic security were taken, including establishment of a cumbersome and costly Department of Homeland Security.

With the support of allies, American forces attacked the Taliban government of Afghanistan, which had provided a refuge and training grounds for Osama Bin Laden, the well-financed terrorist leader, who had planned and organized the attack. The training camps were destroyed and an extensive search for Bin Laden and his followers was undertaken in the rugged mountains of Afghanistan and Pakistan. Plans were announced to establish a new government in Afghanistan and rebuild the country, which had been devastated by twenty years of war and several years of Taliban rule. Judging from the past, the prospects for this quixotic scheme were not good.

More important for America and the Bush administration was the invasion of Iraq, which provided a classic example of hubris [overweening pride] and abuse of military power. From the beginning of the Bush administration in 2001, planning had begun to invade Iraq and overthrow Saddam Hussein. A pretext was found in the horrifying events of Sept. 11, 2001 and the national outrage that followed. Although Saddam Hussein had nothing to do with the terrorist attack, and was, in fact, an enemy of Moslem fundamentalists, Bush declared that Saddam's presumed weapons of mass destruction must be destroyed as part of "the war on terror."

A diplomatic dance took place, as the Bush administration attempted to obtain authorization from a reluctant United Nations to invade Iraq. In November 2002, the Security Council agreed to give Saddam "a final opportunity" to admit U. N. inspectors. Saddam agreed and the inspectors began their inspections. In January 2003, the administration began deployment of 62,000 American troops to the Persian Gulf; many of them were stationed in Kuwait. With an armed force in readiness, the White House and the Defense Department wanted to attack as soon as possible. The United Nations and America's most important friends and allies saw no immediate justification for invading Iraq. Britain and Australia sent troops, but Canada did not. The inspections were progressing and the inspectors had found nothing, but in mid-March 2003 Bush declared that he could wait no longer and invaded anyway.

This time the goal was "regime change" followed by establishment of democracy in Iraq and hopefully throughout the Arab world. The U. S.

Army, led by the Third Infantry Division, performed well against minimal resistance. Baghdad was captured, Saddam was overthrown, and the American television audience cheered, little thinking the United States was now confronted with the problems (daunting) and costs (unsupportable) of rebuilding Iraq and creating a new government in a country with deep-seated ethnic and religious divisions and a long-standing resentment of Western interference. Bush asked Congress for $87 billion for the occupation and reconstruction of Iraq in the next year. Presumably these heavy expenditures will continue for several years. The world may have been better off without Saddam Hussein, but the people of the United States definitely were not.

On May 1, 2004 Bush declared that the war was at an end. He described it as "a crucial advance in the campaign against terror." Since there was no evidence that Iraq was involved in terrorism, the Iraq War must tentatively be assessed as a misuse of American military power and an abuse of the trust and loyalty of the American people. However, it made a good TV show, and Bush presented himself as a strong "war president" who had acted decisively to protect the security of the United States.

With an eye toward the presidential election, Bush announced that the United States would surrender "sovereignty" to an interim Iraqi government on June 30, 2004. The interim government—in contradiction to the usual meaning of the word "sovereignty"—would have no power. Its only responsibilities would be to supervise public administration and organize elections to be held in 2005. An expensively trained police for of Iraqis was expected to maintain order, but it was doubtful that they would hold together when confronted with challenges from their countrymen. More than 100,000 American troops would remain in the area to maintain American authority and intervene, if necessary. A huge American embassy, well stocked with CIA agents trained in counter-terrorism, would "advise" the government from behind the scenery. Presumably, U. S. and foreign firms are waiting in the wings to share the bonanza expected from reconstruction contracts and oil production. These steps are intended to enable Bush to face the American electorate in November as a leader who waged a victorious war and made a durable peace.

Assessment

It is evident that the Bush administration has committed itself to "big government Conservatism" at home, large expenditures for advanced weapons systems, and an active foreign policy. These policies cannot long be sustained by the accumulation of debt, although the system may last long enough to get Bush reelected in November 2004. The American people are beginning to realize that they were conned into the Iraq War, which turned out to be much more costly in lives, money, and long-term commitments than they were led to expect. A sluggish economic recovery, characterized by a weak job market and low investment (i. e., lack of confidence in the long-term future) is becoming disturbing. The United States, in contrast to its history and ideals, is developing an "hour-glass" economy, with a bulge of wealth at the top and a bulge of poverty at the bottom, while the middle class—the bedrock of our democracy—is squeezed. America's massive trade deficits and the fall of the dollar in international money markets may have some short-term advantages, but the disadvantages are already being seen in higher energy prices that could derail our faltering recovery. America is a strong country and can take a lot of abuse, but sooner or later, the chickens will come home to roost.

Epilogue

America was founded on Liberal principles, and Liberals have taken the lead in bringing America to its present greatness. They must continue to believe that freedom works while making certain that it works for everyone.

Principles

Faced with the challenges of the twenty-first century and the alternative vision of America presented by the new Conservatives, it is incumbent on Liberals to identify their principles and articulate them to a nation engulfed by a cacophony of voices and television images. This book is intended to contribute to that process.

The first step is to make America a shining light of Liberal Democracy. The reader of this book already knows what that means. It would be an error of the first magnitude to sacrifice that goal to global ambitions or domestic partisanship and pressure groups. The doctrine of Liberal Realism enunciated in this book should lead Liberals to take all grand schemes, at home or abroad, with a grain or two of salt.

The next point is to recognize that a unique combination of circumstances has put the United States in a position of world leadership with great potential for good or ill. The United States is the center of "globalization": the movement of people, money, goods and ideas throughout the world. Globalization is made possible by changes in communications and transportation, and has led to increasing economic interdependence. Not all parts of the world share fully in the process, and Liberal Realism requires an understanding of the diverse peoples, nations, religions and cultures that make up the human family. Nevertheless, America must be the dynamic core of the emerging world community. America has the energy and imagination to thrive in our globalizing world, and it would be damaging to our future to throttle our most creative minds and industries by using our talents and resources to fight wars around the world.

The world community has developed a complex network of international and regional organizations, and the United States should support these institutions to the extent that they contribute to peace, prosperity, and mutual understanding. That will require some concessions to the wishes and needs of others. The United States would be a big loser if the international order that Liberals have worked to achieve broke down, as it did in the 1930s.

Balanced budgets are essential to maintain confidence in America's long-term economic future, and confidence in the future is essential to encourage innovation and investment. The dollar remains the international medium of exchange. For that reason it is essential to maintain a strong and stable dollar, and that requires fiscal and monetary responsibility. Liberals must be willing to tax to meet current and future needs; the American economy cannot grow by the accumulation of debt.

In a highly competitive world, it is important to reduce the tax burden on the productive part of the economy (employers, workers) and shift it more to incomes and wealth. It is only fair that those who benefit the most from America should pay the most to keep this great country thriving. Liberals should also have the courage to cut unwarranted subsidies and wasteful spending, despite the cries of those who have found a place at the public trough. Borrowing may be necessary on occasion, but it should be accompanied by provisions to pay the interest and eventually retire the debt.

America is the world's premier military power, and this power should be used to maintain a peaceful, orderly world. Our military forces should be tailored in size, cost, and functions to fit foreseeable needs. Militarism for its own sake or to intimidate others has always been a temptation to powerful states, and the United States is not immune to that mentality. Liberals should not be reluctant to use our military power when it is clearly needed, but it should be used with restraint and with respect to international institutions and the views of other countries.

As much as possible in a popular democracy, where many interests clash, we must try to keep our constitutional structure and electoral process open to reason and discussion and free of the corruption of money. It is difficult to think of a way to limit the pernicious effects of television campaigning while preserving television as an important medium for the discussion of public affairs. Nevertheless, something must be done. At present, the corruption of politics by money and television advertising seems to be our fatal flaw, and Liberals should fight it on all fronts.

We must maintain a working balance between federal, state, and local governments. Federal funding and standards should be combined with state and local administration of many of our social services. In the twentieth century, Liberals extended the role of government to deal with our most pressing social needs. They must fight to preserve these gains from destruction by under-funding or repeal.

America is also a civilization and an important contributor to the emerging world civilization. Governmental appropriations and charitable contributions are needed to maintain and improve our educational and cultural institutions. Liberals are advocates of freedom but they are not libertarians, and some restraints must be maintained on the excesses of commercialized popular culture. The evils of crime, drugs, vandalism, abusive relationships, and terrorism must be fought with vigor. The support of an enlightened, energized public opinion will be necessary to keep America a good place to live and work.

Agenda

The liberal agenda for the election of 2004 should include support of international institutions, good relations with allies and other friendly countries, restraint in the use of force in the zones of instability, a tax policy based on ability to pay that provides adequate revenue to meet genuine national needs, careful pruning of unwarranted tax breaks and subsidies, long-needed reforms in the cost and structures of our military forces, an important federal role in funding education, health care, and law enforcement while delegating many administrative responsibilities to the states, protection of the environment, stronger control of immigration without obstructing needlessly the flow of those immigrants who are important to our economy, and vigilance in defending personal Liberty against meretricious claims of national security.

America was founded on Liberal principles, and Liberals have taken the lead in bringing America to its present greatness. They must continue to believe that freedom works while making certain that it works for everyone.

0-595-30369-2